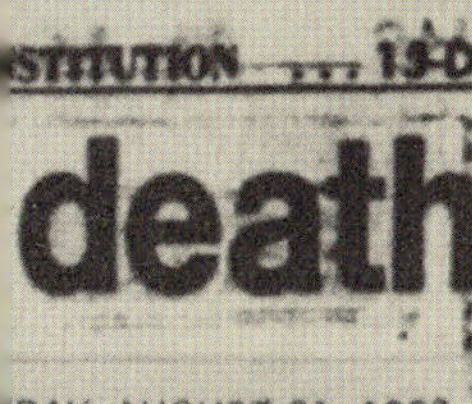



**death**

# Contras hit another ferry to Bluefields

## Sandinistas on board repel attack, call it an attempt to cut off region

# Mystery deepens over US man shot down in Nicaragua

MYSTERY still surrounds the US citizen captured on Sunday by the Nicaraguan government when

From Scott Wallace in Managua

"volunteers" said to belong to the Alabama-based Civilian Military Assistance group which shares

# Guerrillas' vow: 'We won't knuckle under'

Despite U.S. and Salvadoran government claims that the guerrillas are on the defensive, a New Year's celebration in Tenancingo finds the rebels in high spirits, confident that time is on their side.

By Scott Wallace

"The other side apparently is not ready. But we won't knuckle under to their de-

# Hot war with no end in sight

**The civil war in El Salvador has intensified, in spite of the thaw in East-West relations. Scott Wallace reports from San Salvador**

**A**T A TIME when peace is breaking out elsewhere, the carnage visited on tiny El Salvador during the past week ing its policy in its traditional "back yard" — Central America.

Gone are the arguments with which Washington's cold war-tion to rise up in support for their offensive.

If the guerrillas hoped their unprecedented attack and week-long occupation of nearly one-third of metropolitan San Salvador would bring the extreme right within the Government and armed forces out the woodwork, they succeede Many here see the assassi tion of Catholic University r the renewed threats mark a return to the early 1980s, when right-wing death squads and security forces spared no one in their witch-hunt of suspected leftists, not even Archbishop Oscar Arnulfo Romero or four American nuns.

THE INDEPENDENT Wednesday 29 October 19

# Death squads heighten crisis for Salvadorans

By Scott Wallace
Special to The Journal-Constitution

SAN SALVADOR, El Salvador — The right-w death squads are back at their bloody work in

# Confessions of a gun-runner

EUGENE HASENFUS has little of the *macho*, gung-ho spirit that ne might expect from an arms rafficker caught in the middle of Central America's political up-eaval.

Since his capture by the Sandi-Eugene Hasenfus, sole survivor of an abortive flight to drop supplies to the Nicarguan Contra rebels, talks in a Managua prison to Scott Wallace of his anger at being 'abandoned' by the US trieve one from his brother.

Similarly, Mr Hasenfus he and his colleagues kept as for copies of the one page tract they had signed with phantom company, Portland

# Central America in the Crosshairs of War

Forced evacuation of peasants, El Ventarrón, Nicaragua, 1985.

# Central America in the Crosshairs of War:
## On the Road from Vietnam to Iraq

**Photographs and Text by Scott Wallace**

with a foreword by the
Honorable Christopher J. Dodd

George F. Thompson Publishing
in association with the
Center for the Study of Place

Survivor of a massacre, Chalatenango, El Salvador, 1984.

For the people of Central America
and my colleagues in journalism
around the world

Para los pueblos de Centroamérica
y mis colegas periodistas
en todas partes del mundo

Leftist guerrillas, Chinameca, El Salvador, 1983.

# CONTENTS


9   FOREWORD *by the Honorable Christopher J. Dodd*

15   INTRODUCTION Coming of Age on the Fields of Battle

25   **A Gallery of Photographs from the Field**

47   ONE   Killer Nights

57   TWO   Ghosts of Vietnam

65   THREE   The Invisible War

75   FOUR   Meet the Rebels

83   FIVE   Gualsinga River

93   SIX   The Element of Surprise

103   SEVEN   The Miskito Coast

113   EIGHT   Hunting Down the Sons of Reagan

123   NINE   Shot Out of Nowhere

133   TEN   End of the Road

141   ELEVEN   In Search of Enemies

155   **Press Credentials**

159   **A Gallery of Field Notes and Radio Scripts**

165   *Notes on the Photographs*

175   *Notes in the Text*

181   *Suggested Readings*

185   *Acknowledgments*

189   *About the Author and the Essayist*

191   *About the Book*

U.S. Senator Christopher Dodd (D-Conn.) speaks with reporters upon arrival in Managua, Nicaragua, in September 1987 on a fact-finding mission. To his right is U.S. Senator John McCain (R-Ariz.) and behind and between Senators Dodd and McCain is U.S. Senator Terry Stanford (D-N.C.). Photograph © Lou Dematteis and used with permission.

**I**t may seem like a long time ago, but the 1980s were a critical period in our nation's history that continues to reverberate in important ways to this day. At the time, the United States was still engaged in a global struggle with the Soviet Union over which system of government and way of life would prevail: democracy or communism. Since direct confrontation between the two superpowers could have led to nuclear war and mutual annihilation, the two nations confronted one another indirectly, by proxy, at flashpoints across the world in a Cold War, where each side sought to promote its values and strategic interests.

Then as now, policy debates in Washington, D.C., over how best to achieve our goals were contentious. Nowhere were disagreements more acute than over U.S. policies on Central America. The region was roiling when Ronald Reagan entered the White House in January 1981. In Nicaragua, the Sandinista National Liberation Front (FSLN) had overthrown a longtime American ally: the Somoza family dictatorship. In neighboring El Salvador, a similarly Marxist-oriented guerrilla movement, the Farabundo Martí National Liberation Front (FMLN), was on the verge of toppling another military regime that had long been friendly with the United States. Intelligence reports indicated that the Sandinistas were furnishing weapons to the FMLN rebels in El Salvador.

On Capitol Hill, there was deep concern on both sides of the aisle that the Soviets were seeking to expand their influence in the Western Hemisphere, representing a potential threat to U.S. national security. President Reagan entered office determined to exert U.S. influence with military power first and foremost, at the expense of core American values. Human rights, social justice, and the rule of law were of secondary interest to the new administration. As Scott Wallace so ably and dramatically illustrates in words and images in this eye-opening volume, the consequences for the people of Central America were devastating.

President Reagan pushed quickly for a dramatic boost in military aid to El Salvador, a country ruled by a government that was murdering its own people to maintain a grotesquely skewed economic order. In Nicaragua, the President instructed the Central Intelligence Agency to create, arm, and train a rebel army, called the Contras, supposedly for the purposes of intercepting weapons flowing from the Sandinistas to Salvadoran guerrillas. Formed from the officer corps of Somoza's National Guard, the Contras' real purpose, at least as they understood it, was to overthrow the Sandinistas and regain power. It wasn't long before the Contras were rampaging through the Nicaraguan countryside, attacking civilian targets and sowing terror. This initial deception was followed by many others as the decade progressed and the Reagan Administration resorted to lies and outright illegalities in pursuit of its aims. In doing so, the President and his supporters displayed a contempt for Congress and the democratic process.

I was elected to my first term in the U.S. Senate in 1980, in the same general election that brought Ronald Reagan to the White House. My understanding of what was happening in El Salvador and Nicaragua was very different from his. While Reagan saw Central America primarily as a place on the Cold War chessboard where he would halt perceived Soviet expansion with military force, my view was grounded in first-hand experience. I had served as a Peace Corps volunteer in the region during the 1960s and had witnessed the grinding poverty and social injustice that characterized daily life for the vast majority of people there. I had gained a deep appreciation for their yearning for change, and I understood that, in Guatemala, Nicaragua, and El Salvador, their democratic aspirations had been repeatedly crushed with force throughout the twentieth century.

Our highest officials displayed an ignorance of realities of Central America on par with the little we knew of Vietnam twenty years earlier. I joined my colleagues in the House and Senate to oppose such militaristic policies, seeking instead for negotiated outcomes to the conflicts that would advance the interests of the people of Central America and the United States. For our efforts, many fellow lawmakers and I were subjected to crude charges of being "soft on communism."

Journalists who got to the frontlines in Central America to see things for themselves reported their findings and provided an invaluable service. Their reports and images—in newspapers and news magazines, on radio and television—gave the American people and their elected officials a much more realistic sense of the true nature of those conflicts. Those reporters not only were instrumental in helping my colleagues in Congress craft alternative policies that promoted America's core interests and values, but they created documentary evidence of immense value today. We can only grapple with our immigration crisis, for example, by understanding its root causes in the Central American proxy wars funded and directed by the United States during the 1980s.

The extraordinary record provided by Scott Wallace with his unique reporting speaks to the heart of what it means to be an American: courageous and compassionate, honest and unflinching. In creating this lasting record, Wallace shows what is possible when we peel away the layers of prejudice and propaganda and strive to see things as they really are. At a time of industrial-scale disinformation and "alternative facts," Scott Wallace highlights the critical importance of enterprising journalists and a free press to society, as protected by the First Amendment. It is my hope that this book will inspire a new generation of journalists to take up the mantle. The survival of democracy will depend on it.

Protest against U.S. support for the Contras, Managua, Nicaragua, 1987.

SWAN ISLANDS

MEXICO
CHIAPAS
Tenosique
Presa de la Angostura
Comitán
La Mesilla
SIERRA
Todos Santos Cuchumatán
Tapachula
SAN MARCOS
Huehuetenango
Quetzaltenango

Lago Petén Itzá
Dos Erres
Flores
PETÉN
Usumacinta
San Pedro
Pasión
Ixcán
HUEHUETENANGO
Sierra de los Cuchumatanes
QUICHÉ
Finca La Perla
Nebaj
Chajul
San Juan Cotzal
Uspantán
GUATEMALA
Santa Cruz del Quiché
MADRE
Guatemala
DE
Cobán
ALTA VERAPAZ
Lago de Izabal
IZABAL
ESCUINTLA
CHIAPAS

BELIZE
Belize City
Belmopan
CAYO
STANN CREEK
TOLEDO

GULF OF HONDURAS
Puerto Barrios
San Pedro Sula
COPÁN
Motagua
SANTA BÁRBARA

ISLAS DE LA BAHÍA
La Ceiba
ATLÁNTIDA
Aguan
YORO
COLÓN
Puerto Castilla
COSTA
DE

CARIBBEAN SEA

Montañas de Comayagua
COMAYAGUA
OLANCHO
El Aguacate
Patuca
GRACIAS A DIOS
Rus Rus
Coco
Puerto Lempira

HONDURAS
FRANCISCO MORAZÁN
Palmerola
EL PARAÍSO
Tegucigalpa
Yamales
La Ladosa
NUEVA SEGOVIA
San Juan del Río Coco
San Lorenzo
MADRIZ
Quilalí
Kilambé
El Ventarrón
Cordillera Isabelia
Bocay
Waspam
Wawa
ZELAYA NORTE
Bonanza
Sukatpin
Siuna
La Rosita
Yulu
Karatá
Haulover
Puerto Ca
Prinzapolka
San José de Bocay
El Cuá
Finca La Sorpresa
ESTELÍ
Tuma
Prinzapolka
Río Grande de Matagalpa
ATLA
OC

PACIFIC OCEAN

see inset for more detail
EL SALVADOR
San Salvador
Ilopango
COASTAL
(LITTORAL)
HWY
Tiger Island

CHINANDEGA
Jinotega
JINOTEGA
Matagalpa
MATAGALPA

Corinto
Momotombo
Lago de Managua
Punta Huete
Managua
Masaya
LEÓN
Santo Tomás
CHONTALES
Cordillera Chontaleña
La Piñuela
Mico
Rama
Escondido
Pearl Lagoon
Bluefields

NICARAGUA

DECADE OF CONFLICT:
CENTRAL AMERICA IN THE 1980s

ZELAYA SUR
Nueva Guinea
Lago de Nicaragua
PAN AMERICAN HWY
Ometepe
San Carlos
RIVAS
San Juan del Nor
ALAJUELA
COSTA RICA
GUANACASTE
San José
SAN JOSÉ
Cordillera de Talam
LIM
PUNTAREN

EL SALVADOR INSET
1:1,850,000
0  10  20 Kilometers
0  10  20 Miles

GUATEMALA
Jutiapa
JUTIAPA
Lago de Güija
Santa Ana
Ahuachapán
AHUACHAPÁN
Izalco
Sonsonate
SONSONATE
Los Mangos
San Salvador
Lago de Coatepeque
Lempa
EL SALVADOR
Vol. de San Salvador
Ilopango
Lago Ilopango
Guadalupe
LA LIBERTAD
Santa Cruz
La Paz
Loma
COASTAL
(LITTORAL)
HWY
Puente de Oro
San Agustín
San Francisco Javier
Jiquilisco
Usulután

Montaña de Celaque
La Palma
CHALATENANGO
Lago Suchitlán
El Zapotal
Las Vueltas
Chalatenango
San Francisco Lempa
Copapayo
Cinquera
Suchitoto
Guazapa
CUSCATLÁN
Tenancingo
San Pedro
Perulapán
CABAÑAS
Cerros de San Pedro
San Lorenzo
San Clara
San Vicente
SAN VICENTE
Chichontepec
Puente Cuscatlán
Estanzuelas
Chinameca
Sta. Elena
Las Marías
Lago de Olomega

HONDURAS
INTIBUCÁ
Palmerola
LEMPIRA
LA PAZ
Perquín
El Mozote
MORAZÁN
San Francisco Gotera
Anamorós
Yamabal
Santa Rosa de Lima
Cacahuatique
San Miguel
SAN MIGUEL
PAN AMERICAN HWY
Chaparrastique
La Unión
LA UNIÓN
Tiger Island
Golfo de Fonseca
Jucuarán
PACIFIC OCEAN

LEGEND
Military Base
Air Base
Listening Post
U.S. Naval Exercises
Bridge
Contra Camp
Clandestine Air Drop to Contras
Refugee Camp
Volcano / Peak
Country Capital
Town
International boundary
Department boundary
Main Road
Other Road

SCALE
1:4,400,000
0  50  100 Kilometers
0  50  100 Miles
Albers Conic Projection
N
Cartography by Rachael H. Carpenter

# Central America
# in the Crosshairs of War

Scott Wallace (left) interviews an unidentified officer of the Sandinista Popular Army on the frontlines, Nueva Segovia, Nicaragua, 1984. Photograph © Bill Gentile and used with permission.

# Coming of Age
# on the Fields of Battle

**I never would have done what I did** if it had not been for Vietnam.

That war shaped my life like no other event, informing decisions I would make for years to come. Like the rest of my generation, I grew up with images of that conflict beamed into our living room on the evening news. I was still in grade school, but those grainy, black-and-white news clips stuck with me: thwapping helicopters swarming a landing zone to the popping of gunfire; suspected Vietcong guerrillas, rounded up, bound, and blindfolded; GIs setting fire to palm-thatched hooches with Zippo lighters while village women frantically tried to douse the flames before they lost everything they owned.

Watching the news was a nightly ritual, long before there was CNN, the Internet, social media. There were only three channels on television: ABC, NBC, and CBS. By far and away, the most trusted in our household was the *CBS Evening News* and its anchorman, Walter Cronkite. I was transfixed, both horrified and fascinated, by the stories from Vietnam that he and the CBS correspondents brought into our home and the names of many of the places they reported from remained lodged in my memory: the A Shau Valley, Da Nang, Dak To.

Our downstairs coffee table was stacked with oversized Time-Life and American Heritage books on the Civil War, the two World Wars, the Cold War. Together, they amounted to a history of photojournalism and war photography. When I was ten, my parents gave me my first camera, a Polaroid Swinger, and a leather-bound diary to record daily life and thoughts. They took me and my two older brothers to see epic productions on the big screen: *Lawrence of Arabia, Doctor Zhivago, Around the World in 80 Days*. And they took us on road trips from our home in upstate New York to Florida to visit relatives along winding, two-lane thoroughfares before Interstate highways homogenized the experience of car travel. It was like magic, moving from the dead of winter with its blowing snowdrifts to the tilled fields and sharecropper shacks of the Carolinas and on to the mysterious backroads of Georgia in the shadow of overhanging boughs bearded with Spanish moss. Travel, photography, writing. My mother and father gave me these gifts and awakened in me a curiosity about the world that one day I would fashion into a career.

By the time we got a color TV, the images from Vietnam were accompanied by scenes of conflict closer to home— confrontations between police and student protestors in the nation's capital and elsewhere. In the Fall of 1969, I left home for boarding school in New England and joined sit-ins on campus the following spring over the deaths of students at Kent State and Jackson State at the hands of National Guardsmen and police. As a freshman at Yale a few years later, I attended the last big march against the war on the National Mall to protest the 1972 Christmas bombing of North Vietnam ordered by President Richard Nixon and Secretary of State Henry Kissinger.

I tried to find my way in a confusing, upside-down time. On a year off from college in 1974, I journeyed to Mexico, learned Spanish, then continued overland to South America, traveling by rail, bus, and on the flatbeds of trucks down the spine of the Andes. I worked as a volunteer literacy teacher in an Indigenous community in the Peruvian Amazon. While in Lima, I stayed in a house leased to the U.N. to shelter refugees from Chile. They were fleeing the brutal military dictatorship of General Augusto Pinochet, who had overthrown the democratically elected socialist president Salvador Allende with the connivance of Nixon and Kissinger, the Pentagon, and the CIA.[1] My Chilean friends—professors, trade unionists, even a professional soccer player—recounted tales of terror and torture at the hands of Pinochet's secret police and their harrowing escape from the country. Their stories were so wildly at odds with Americans' view of the U.S.A. as a shining light on a hill, a promoter of freedom and democracy, that I began to wonder if what we had done in Vietnam, and the lying and dissembling our leaders engaged in about it, were more the norm than an aberration.

In 1979, the Sandinistas rode a popular insurrection to power in Nicaragua, toppling the U.S.-backed Somoza family dictatorship and sending shockwaves across the hemisphere. Full-scale civil war erupted the following year in neighboring El Salvador, as a mass movement took up arms in response to decades of abuse under a murderous military and rapacious oligarchy. By then I was living in New York City, bouncing between jobs, still unsure of a career path. Slowly, an idea took shape: Maybe I could become a journalist and report those stories myself. But how? I decided to enroll in graduate school, at the University of Missouri, to learn the trade. If I were going to Central America, I knew I'd have to go as a freelancer; no news organization would hire a novice straight out of school and send him out to cover a big international story, particularly one that entailed a high degree of danger. To make it as an independent journalist, I would have to

acquire as broad a range of skills as possible. At Missouri I took an eclectic mix of courses to cover all the bases: newspaper writing, radio and television reporting, photojournalism.

During my two years in journalism school, Central America roiled. President Ronald Reagan took office in 1981 vowing to "draw the line against communist aggression" in El Salvador. Aid from the U.S. began to pour into El Salvador, despite the government's horrifying record of death-squad terror and battlefield massacres. Reagan signed a national security directive to arm and direct Nicaragua's rightwing rebels, called the "Contras," supposedly to interdict alleged weapons shipments from the Sandinistas to the Salvadoran guerrillas. America's national security was at stake, the White House proclaimed, as the U.S. launched a war by proxy in both El Salvador and Nicaragua. America would put up the money, the training, and the weapons. The "little brown men," as the top U.S. military advisor called the local forces, would do the dying.[2] His words carried an eerie echo from twenty years earlier, when then-Secretary of Defense Robert McNamara dismissed our Viet Cong adversaries as "little men in black pajamas." As with Vietnam, officials in Washington similarly saw the world as a global chessboard, the U.S. vying with the Soviet Union (U.S.S.R.) for supremacy, with little understanding of the history and conditions that had given rise to revolution in Central America. I decided I would do what I could to rectify that ignorance, at least in the minds of U.S. taxpayers and voters. El Salvador was where I would plant my flag.

Shortly before graduation from Missouri, I met CBS News executives when they visited the campus. At network headquarters in New York City a month later, I was introduced to a gruff, silver-haired man as he stood amid a maze of gray metal desks and barked orders over the clatter of typewriters and telex machines. Larry McCoy, the executive editor of CBS News Radio, sized me up through narrowed eyes. "El Salvador, huh?" he said and took a puff on his pipe.

"I don't have anyone there at the moment. Just the damned TV people who send something when I lean on them." He strode over to a telex machine, a kind of standup typewriter that pounded out a ceaseless stream of reports from the newswires: Associated Press (AP), United Press International (UPI), Reuters. McCoy yanked a ten-foot-stretch of paper from the machine, tore off a dozen news stories from the scroll, and handed them to me: "Rewrite these as thirty-second news spots, then voice them. You have a tape recorder, right? Good. FedEx the tape to me from the road. Call me collect when you get to Miami."

McCoy got the tape and liked what he heard. I would be the CBS News "stringer," or freelance reporter, in El Salvador. He told me to stop at the CBS bureau in Miami, where I was issued CBS press credentials and radio gear—a professional Sony cassette deck, mic, and a set of "alligator clips" to connect the tape machine to a telephone receiver, the standard method for filing radio stories across an international phone line. Just as importantly, I had authorization to work out of the CBS bureau in San Salvador, El Salvador's capital. Before leaving the U.S., I worked out a separate deal to file articles and photographs as the stringer for *The Atlanta Journal-Constitution*. I arrived in El Salvador on June 18, 1983, a newly minted j-school graduate eager to cover the big story.

I wasn't the only one who had this idea. For a generation of post-Vietnam, post-Watergate journalists arriving in Central America during the early 1980s, the armed conflicts in El Salvador and Nicaragua—and, to a lesser extent, Guatemala— were to become the crucible where we learned our trade and forged our careers. Many of us—the freelancers, in particular—arrived as idealists, with a passionate conviction that we could make a difference. Twenty years earlier, U.S. officials from the President on down ignored warning signs that propping up the corrupt government of South Vietnam was a lost cause that would lead to disaster. Perhaps this time we could help head off a catastrophe before it happened. After all, the

United States was playing a major role in all three conflicts, especially in El Salvador and Nicaragua, and public opinion mattered to American officials and lawmakers. That made us, the purveyors of the news, pivotal to the equation. And Vietnam had made many of us more skeptical, less willing to take official pronouncements at face value.

I quickly picked up on the more superficial likenesses between El Salvador and Vietnam. There was an unquestionable familiarity about the barefoot peasants stooped under crushing loads, the soldiers in camouflage fanning out across smoldering fields, the anguished wails of bereaved wives and mothers. Green Berets, mostly Vietnam veterans, were training local forces in the arts of unconventional war, and guerrillas were staging punishing attacks before melting back into the jungle. In Washington, officials dusted off the old domino theory that envisioned all Southeast Asia falling to the Communists, one domino at a time, if South Vietnam didn't hold the line. This time, President Reagan warned, the proximity of Central America heightened the stakes all the more, raising the specter of the "Red menace" rolling north to the banks of the Río Grande.

The more covert parallels were not as obvious but no less salient. The secrecy and duplicity that guided much of U.S. policy in Southeast Asia were finally laid bare by the publication in 1971 of the Pentagon Papers by *The New York Times* and *The Washington Post*, vindicating the young reporters who had spoken truth to power from the earliest days of the war. Likewise, it was after a clandestine resupply flight to the Contras was shot down over Nicaragua in late 1986 that an Independent Counsel for Iran/Contra Matters was able to peel back some of the most deeply hidden layers of the illegality and deception that lay at the core of Washington's machinations in Central America.

I aimed to witness what was happening with my own eyes and ears and share my findings with the public back in the States. I had no idea how long I would stay, but it was going to be long enough to dive in deep. I hadn't come to build a portfolio of exotic datelines. I did not think of it as steppingstone on my way to somewhere else or to further career ambitions. But I did revel in the adventure, drawn to the allure of the open road. I had, in a way, burned the ship that had brought me to shore, precluding an early return. I'd abandoned my old '66 Chevy Impala in a Miami parking lot and left the keys with a friend if he wanted to take it away. I had scraped together the funds for a one-way ticket and had just $50 in cash to my name.

On the photography side of my fledgling enterprise, I started out with a single Nikkormat 35mm camera. In a Miami photo shop, I stocked up on a mix of color and black-and-white film before leaving the States: Kodachrome, Ektachrome, Tri-X, and Plus-X. To economize, I bought a bunch of Agfachrome, cheaper than Kodak's chrome films, but I would find out later that its dyes deteriorated with the passage of time. I eventually acquired a second camera and thereafter kept one loaded with color, the other with black and white. I tended to favor black and white; the film could be quickly processed in one of the makeshift darkrooms set up in the bathrooms of the AP or UPI bureaus at the Camino Real Hotel in San Salvador, which served as a kind of command central for all the major news organizations covering the war.

The very accommodating newswire photographers would develop my film, then quickly take a blow dryer to the negative strips as they hung from the shower-curtain rod. They would print the image in chemical trays laid out under a safe light on the bathroom counter, then send it out on a rotating drum transmitter that took up to twenty minutes to complete. In this manner, many of the stories I wrote for *The Atlanta Journal-Constitution* and other publications were accompanied by my photographs. The hurried and slapdash nature of the process accounts for the graininess evident in some of the images.* I sent out the text for those stories from the CBS bureau via a telex machine.

Working for both print and broadcast media, I evolved a somewhat eclectic reporting style in the field. At times I'd raise my camera and snap the shutter if I wanted to capture a fleeting moment before it vanished. I found that the camera could sometimes help me enter the space of strangers and engage them first before pulling out my notebook and pen. Sometimes it was the other way around. I'd nearly always seek a subject's tacit permission, establishing eye contact as I moved into position. I was honest and upfront about what I was doing, no subterfuge or sneakiness. I acquired a 20mm wide-angle lens, which allowed me to get more visual information into the frame despite the distortions that would sometimes result, and it forced me to move in even closer to my subjects.

An offer to hand out Polaroid photos also proved to be an excellent icebreaker, a trick I learned from *Time* photographer Bob Nickelsberg. But it wasn't until after my father gave me his old SX-70 when I was home for a visit that I could make the *fotos al minuto* that helped smooth the approach to prospective subjects. If a source's voice resonated with emotion that would make for powerful radio, I would pull out the microphone and roll tape. Before long I also became a scout and de facto field producer for the *CBS Evening News*, leading Dan Rather's visiting correspondents to locations where I knew we would likely find the rebels, the army, or something else of interest. Writing stories for print, taking photographs, recording and voicing for radio, I was an early practitioner of what came to be known as "convergence journalism." Amused colleagues who saw me multitasking in the field called me the "robo-journalist."

We enjoyed access to the competing sides in a way that few other frontline reporters ever did or have since. The fortunes of the belligerent forces were inextricably linked to the images each projected to far-off audiences who neither spoke their language nor had firsthand knowledge of their hopes and struggles. Nevertheless, by virtue of their own governments' power to furnish or withhold arms, training and

*All photographs in this were originally shot on and recently digitized fo art reproduction.

intelligence to the warring factions, the people of the United States and, to a lesser extent, Europe constituted a parallel theater of engagement. As the intermediaries between the shooting war and the information war, we journalists were in the crosshairs—the targets of lies, pressure, and propaganda from all sides. But we also enjoyed a thin layer of protection; anyone who killed a journalist, especially a foreign journalist, would have to answer to higher-ups. Few commanders wanted to deal with that kind of public-relations imbroglio. That didn't keep journalists from dying, but there was a system of accountability that discouraged the wanton targeting of reporters.

In Vietnam, few, if any, American journalists ever attempted to hook up with the Viet Cong. It was inconceivable. It would have been considered treason and could well have been suicidal. And once the escalation began in earnest in 1965, Vietnam became an American story, a story about Americans in Vietnam. It was not about the Vietnamese, not even those who were on "our side." The Viet Cong and the peasant civilians (from whom they were largely indistinguishable) remained an inscrutable enemy, easy to discount and dehumanize.

Like many others covering the conflicts, I was fluent in Spanish. I could speak to the actors on all sides—peasants, politicians, soldiers, guerrillas, even heads of state. Especially for journalists who knew Spanish or made a reasonable effort to speak it, there was a cultural affinity with our Latino hosts that guaranteed a certain level of understanding, even with hardcore revolutionaries who vowed a bloodbath if the Yankees invaded. Despite the concerted efforts by the Reagan Administration and its Republican allies in Congress to demonize the FMLN in El Salvador or the Sandinistas in Nicaragua, we got to know the putative "enemies" well enough and provided enough coverage of their views and actions to assure they would not be a faceless foe, like the Viet Cong had largely been.

As historically occurs with any major foreign policy initiative, particularly an unpopular or controversial one, the Reagan Administration dispatched a series of high-profile emissaries and fact-finding missions to the region. Their visits signaled support for friendly forces and "resolve" to counter the perceived Soviet threat. They also helped create the impression that policy decisions were calibrated, appropriate, well-informed. The parade of dignitaries included Defense Secretary Caspar Weinberger, who was accompanied by then-Major General Colin Powell, seen behind Weinberger wearing his U.S. Army Garrison cap (page 20, left); U.S. Ambassador to the United Nations Jean Kirkpatrick with then-U.S. Ambassador to El Salvador Thomas Pickering (page 20, right); Secretary of State George Schultz; and then-Vice President George H. W. Bush. Sometimes they had something to say that was newsworthy. But for the most part, I felt that my time was better spent out in the field, where the real human drama was unfolding.

A few months into what would become a seven-year assignment in Central America, I had the chance to put a question to Henry Kissinger on the tarmac of El Salvador's Ilopango Airbase (page 21). He had just arrived as head of the "President's National Bipartisan Commission on Central America" to put his imprimatur on Reagan's policies and win support for them in Congress. Despite Kissinger's role in the secret bombing of Cambodia and the illegal wiretaps of White House staff in the Watergate scandal, he had shared a Nobel Prize for negotiating the end of the Vietnam War and still enjoyed wide popularity in Washington. At the time of his visit, the Reagan Administration was touting elections as the answer to El Salvador's deep social ills. The Salvadoran rebels should just lay down their weapons and join the democratic process, the official line went. It didn't matter that the rebels had taken up arms in the first place because of a long history of stolen elections and bloody repression and because they could not campaign safely in a country where their killers

U.S. Secretary of Defense Casper Weinberger at an outdoor press conference, San Vicente, El Salvador, 1983.

U.S. Ambassador to the United Nations Jeane Kirkpatrick (center) arrives by helicopter to investigate charges of a rebel massacre, Santa Cruz Loma, La Paz Department, El Salvador, 1985.

went unpunished. The Kissinger Commission's preordained role was merely to add a veneer of credibility to this unworkable policy.

"Mr. Kissinger," I shouted across the runway over the roar of jet engines. "Given what the U.S. did to democratically elected governments in Guatemala and Chile, why should the people of El Salvador believe the U.S. is truly committed to free and fair elections here?"[3] Kissinger paused to weigh this bit of impertinence from an upstart reporter. "We will issue our report," he said, "and the results will speak for themselves."

The results contributed to another nine years of bloodletting before the war came to an end in El Salvador. An estimated 75,000 lost their lives, and the U.N.-appointed Truth Commission attributed eighty-five percent of assassinations and murders to the military and their death-squad associates.[4] A million Salvadorans would be displaced, half of whom ended up in the United States, mostly as undocumented immigrants. The MS-13 crime syndicate that today plagues cities and suburbs from Los Angeles to Long Island owes its origins to refugees driven north by the violence that the U.S. supported during the 1980s.[5]

It would be another seven years after Kissinger's visit until the guns of the Contra War fell silent in Nicaragua, not before more than 30,000 were killed. It wasn't until 1996 that Peace Accords were finally signed in Guatemala. All told, nearly 200,000 lost their lives in the Guatemalan Civil War, which began in 1960, including 100,000 Indigenous Mayan villagers in the genocidal decade of the 1980s alone. The devastation left these countries in shambles, their social fabric stretched beyond the breaking point. The reverberations from the wanton bloodletting helped nurture a criminal culture that has fused more recently with drug traffickers moving their wares north from the Andes. Today, the countries that make up Central America's Northern Triangle—Guatemala, El Salvador, Honduras—have higher rates of violent death than they did during the wars of the 1980s under both the Reagan and George H. W. Bush presidencies.

Henry Kissinger (center, in the dark suit) is greeted by U.S. and Salvadoran officials, Ilopango Airbase, El Salvador, 1983.

When Ronald Reagan took office in 1981, the U.S. was still licking its wounds from the defeat in Vietnam. It was in Central America during the 1980s that the champions of executive privilege and imperial power snuffed out the reforms meant to rein in the excesses of Vietnam, Watergate, and covert action at home and abroad. The Reagan Administration circumvented congressional oversights put in place after Vietnam by secretly trading arms for hostages and using the proceeds to fund a clandestine war in Nicaragua. After special prosecutor Lawrence Walsh won convictions or guilty pleas of several key players in the Iran-Contra scheme, among them then-Lieutenant Colonel Oliver North, they either got off on technicalities or were pardoned by President George H. W. Bush on his way out of the White House.[6] Walsh told me in an unpublished interview that Bush pardoned Casper Weinberger as an "act of cowardice," because he knew he'd be called to testify under oath in Weinberger's trial about his knowledge of the secret war in Nicaragua. With his pardon of Weinberger, Bush managed to avoid ever having to provide sworn testimony about the deliberate efforts to mislead Congress and the American public during the Reagan years.

By the end of the 1980s, America had come nearly full circle. The U.S. invasion came not in El Salvador or Nicaragua, where it was most expected, but in Panama to remove strongman Manuel Noriega. Officials would later acknowledge that the Panama invasion served as a dress rehearsal for "regime change" and the invasion of Iraq.[7] By the time of the Iraq invasion in 2003, the chastening lessons of Vietnam had been largely forgotten. U.S. military action was made to seem—once again—like a good idea, with calamitous and far-reaching consequences.

In the 1980s, war and indiscriminate terror that was largely funded by the U.S. drove Central Americans by the hundreds of thousands to seek refuge in Los Angeles and other North American cities. Untold numbers of those immigrants were vulnerable, undocumented children orphaned by the violence. They adopted the ways of gang culture to survive. Then, during the 1990s, tens of thousands of them were rounded up and deported back to their home countries, where they regrouped as hybrid, transnational gangs that have wreaked much of the havoc that is driving the more recent waves of immigration north to the United States.

What happened in the backwoods and on the streets of El Salvador, Nicaragua, and Guatemala remains largely unearthed and unexamined. It is time we take a closer look, lest history repeat itself yet again.

As I write, 100 days before an especially consequential U.S. presidential election in 2024, Nicaragua is ruled by the thuggish Daniel Ortega and his eccentric, star-gazing wife, Rosario Murillo. Ortega led the Sandinista government that the U.S. sought to remove. He was voted out of office in 1990, effectively ending the Sandinista Revolution. But he later won a series of elections and has now set himself up as president-for-life presiding over a de facto police state.

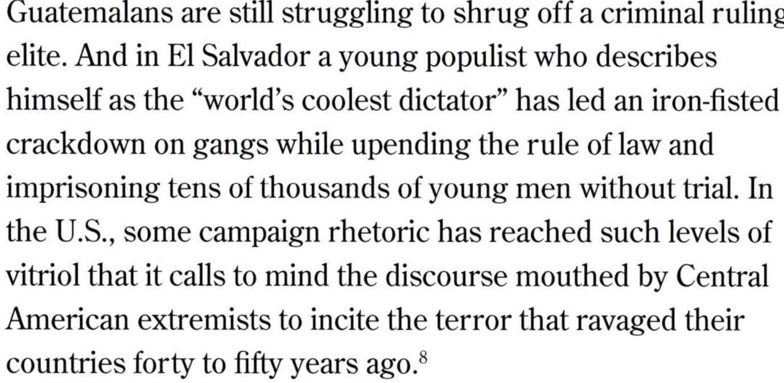

Scott Wallace interviews government soldiers, Quebrada Seca,
San Vicente Department, El Salvador, July 1983.

Photojournalists bide time at a river crossing, Estelí Department,
Nicaragua, 1984.

Guatemalans are still struggling to shrug off a criminal ruling elite. And in El Salvador a young populist who describes himself as the "world's coolest dictator" has led an iron-fisted crackdown on gangs while upending the rule of law and imprisoning tens of thousands of young men without trial. In the U.S., some campaign rhetoric has reached such levels of vitriol that it calls to mind the discourse mouthed by Central American extremists to incite the terror that ravaged their countries forty to fifty years ago.[8]

As a journalist who has covered international events since I first arrived in El Salvador in 1983, I have come to acknowledge a profoundly sad truth: To understand how the catastrophe of Vietnam led to the most recent disasters of Afghanistan and Iraq, one must remember what happened in Central America during the 1980s. In words and images, this book is my effort to reboot our memories and present those tragic events in a new light. It would be worth asking ourselves, for example: What might have happened if we had embraced the desires of Central Americans to build more just, democratic, and equitable societies? What if we had promoted efforts to make their homelands more peaceable and more livable, rather than propping up criminal oligarchies and militaries that sought to stifle change no matter the cost?

I hope this work will provoke renewed debate on such questions. And that members of the press, the public, and aspiring practitioners of journalism, mass media and photography will find value in this account of a reporter coming of age in these important but largely forgotten wars.

Scott Wallace (left) and fellow journalists with guerrilla escorts, Sumpul River, El Salvador, 1984.

Protest against political killings, San Salvador, El Salvador, 1983.

**W**hile covering the conflicts in Central America from 1983 to 1990, I frequently came into contact with people in decisive moments in their lives. Whether I was photographing a brave young boy marching in San Salvador to protest the abduction of his father by death squads or Nicaraguan soldiers boarding helicopters that would carry them over jungles infested with rebels armed with heat-seeking missiles, the sense of urgency and human drama was often inescapable.

Few subjects in these images had the luxury of taking even a day of life on this Earth for granted. As one Nicaraguan officer on the frontlines put it to me: "If there's something you've got to do, don't wait till tomorrow. One moment you're here, the next you're gone. That's what life is like here."

It didn't hurt that I spoke Spanish. Still, the cameras I pointed in their direction could seem intrusive, even if they did confer a reason for my being there. I learned from more experienced photographers. I watched how they moved around a scene, engaged with their subjects and gained their trust, sometimes in just a split second. Perhaps in recognition of the tenuousness of their lives, many of the people who appear in these images seemed to understand, even to take some comfort in my presence, sensing the photographs I was making would be shared with people far away and impart greater meaning to the moment and their loss. Mostly, I was welcomed with graciousness and hospitality.

This gallery includes images of the perpetrators of violence as well as innocent bystanders whose lives were irretrievably shattered in a violent instant. But even amid war and unspeakable horror, the people of Central America found moments of whimsy, as witnessed by the carnival-goers parading in masquerade through a war-ravaged town, and of celebration, like the newlyweds in colorful procession through a long-suffering Indigenous community in the Western Highlands of Guatemala.

It is my hope that, in raising my camera and pressing the shutter, I was able to do some measure of justice to the people I encountered and that I succeeded in capturing and communicating an essential dignity and humanity that transcend the passage of time.

Death-squad suspect, Los Mangos, El Salvador, 1984.

Salvadoran Army officer, Santa Elena, El Salvador, 1984.

Guerrilla militiaman, El Zapotal, El Salvador, 1984.

Revolutionary priest with leftist guerrillas, Jucuarán, El Salvador, 1983.

Carnival, Estanzuelas, El Salvador, 1984.

Indigenous Civil Defense patrol, Todos Santos Cuchumatán, Guatemala, 1983.

Family sugar mill, Uspantán, Guatemala, 1983.

Lieutenant Colonel Domingo Monterrosa (left) addresses Salvadoran Army troops, Santa Elena, El Salvador, 1984.

President José Napoleón Duarte (center) at the funeral for Lieutenant Colonel Domingo Monterrosa, San Salvador, El Salvador, 1984.

Aftermath of a massacre, Chalatenango, El Salvador, 1984.

Guerrilla fighters, Tenancingo, El Salvador, 1985.

Peasant laborers, El Zapotal, El Salvador, 1984.

Tending to a civilian casualty, Las Marías, El Salvador, 1984.

Widow with her bereaved family, San Francisco Lempa, El Salvador, 1983.

Election Day, Jiquilisco, El Salvador, 1989.

Sandinista farming cooperative, Estelí Department, Nicaragua, 1986.

Volunteer *brigadistas* at a security briefing, Finca La Sorpresa, Nicaragua, 1986.

Wedding procession, San Juan Cotzal, Guatemala, 1989.

Adolescent guerrilla fighter, San Francisco Javier, El Salvador, 1989.

Funeral honor guard, San Salvador, El Salvador, 1983.

# ONE

# Killer Nights



**W**e sped through downtown in a torrential downpour, CBS driver Nelson Ayala clutching the wheel to keep us on the road. Shuttered storefronts shot past in a rain-streaked blur. It was just an hour past sunset, but it already felt way too late to be out on the street in this part of San Salvador.

A body appeared in the headlights just ahead of us, sprawled belly-up on the curb. "Jesus!" I shouted. Nelson swerved and kept going. "Shouldn't we stop to help?" I asked. "Not a good idea," he said with a wag of the finger. "You don't know who that person might be or why he is there. We'll call an ambulance from the house."

I'd just arrived in El Salvador that afternoon, my first assignment as a professional journalist. I'd been reading up on the conflict while in journalism school, but I had little idea of what I was getting into. I'd gone straight from the airport to the Camino Real Hotel, where all the foreign press had their bureaus. I didn't have enough money to book a room for even a single night there, but I did have the gear and credentials from CBS News. Nelson, whom I met in the network's bureau at the Camino, offered to put me up until I could get on my feet and find a place of my own.

He steered his van into his garage, just down the street from the lifeless body. We climbed the stairs to the second floor, past piles of sand and exposed steel rebar. The house was still under construction, Nelson explained. He went to the phone and made a call. He did not offer his name. Then he flipped off the lights, and we went to the window. Minutes later, an ambulance silently approached, its red strobe flashing off the wet pavement. Two silhouetted figures hopped out, bundled the body into the back, and drove off.

"You have to be careful," Nelson admonished, stepping back from the window. "That person is dead for a reason. Stay away from dead people if you don't want to end up that way yourself."

Nelson Ayala had experience in such matters. For the past two years, he'd been ferrying CBS crews everywhere news broke: firefights, funerals, embassy briefings. It was work that aroused no small amount of suspicion in a place like El Salvador, where foreign journalists were seen by many as enemies of the state and were routinely exhorted to *tell the truth!* by those who believed we did not. As if that did not make him enough of a target, he had also invested in two buses that ran the busy interurban route between San Salvador and Santa Tecla. Mass transit, Nelson explained, was the object of frequent guerrilla boycotts. If he defied the traffic bans, his buses could be firebombed. If he heeded the rebels' warnings and kept his buses off the road, he risked the appearance of collaborating with the subversives.

I guessed Nelson was in his early thirties. His dark skin, thin mustache, and stocky build gave him the look of a mestizo Sancho Panza. His parental manner suggested there was a lesson to be learned in everything he had to say. He went to his nightstand and retrieved a snub nose revolver from the drawer. From the same drawer, Nelson retrieved a stack of letters, all unsigned, all typed with the same upper-case message: "WE KNOW WHAT YOU ARE UP TO." He wasn't sure what they knew or what they thought they knew. "Anything can get you in trouble here," he said. The threats were likely linked to the CBS work, he figured, because he was also getting menacing phone calls. A taunting voice said, "Columbia Pictures? Columbia Pictures?" followed by a mirthless laugh before the line went dead. I took me a second, but then I got the reference to the Columbia Broadcasting System. CBS.

At the airport that afternoon, I'd hopped a cheap *colectivo*, a microbus, for the trip into the city. It was packed with disheveled men in their twenties and thirties. They had just arrived from Houston, where they said they'd been nabbed by *la migra,* U.S. immigration authorities, and deported. Some of them had no luggage, others small vinyl gym bags or pillowcases stuffed with a few meager belongings. Their banter was surprisingly cheerful as we cruised up the highway. But a hush fell over them as we approached the shanty-towns etched into steep hillsides on San Salvador's outskirts. We stopped every mile or so to let someone off. He'd muster a brave smile and wave goodbye. These men had sought to escape the vice-grip of war: death squads, forced recruitment, random violence. But here they were, back again. I wondered what fate would befall them.

Only the day before, I'd been lounging poolside in Miami's Coconut Grove. Now I was bedding down on a bare mattress on the floor of a half-built house in a gritty, working-class district of San Salvador, by far the most violent city in the hemisphere. The body on the street outside, the deportees, Nelson's predicament—it was a lot to take in on a first day. As I dozed off into a fitful sleep, it occurred to me that I'd already seen a side of Nelson, and of El Salvador, that might have escaped my notice altogether if I hadn't been forced to start out on a shoestring.

Despite its tiny size, El Salvador had become a top U.S. national security priority since 1980, when full-scale civil war broke out. It pitted a murderous military and rapacious oligarchy against a popular movement that had radicalized into an armed insurgency that posed a serious threat to the status quo. Fearing El Salvador would "go the way of Nicaragua," where a leftist guerrilla movement had toppled a pro-U.S. dictatorship in 1979, the Carter Administration in its final days threw its support behind the brutal Salvadoran government, committing $5 million in emergency funding. Despite concerns over its abysmal human-rights record, President Carter's decision set the stage for a far more enthusiastic embrace of the regime by the Reagan Administration. By the time of my arrival, El Salvador was on its way to becoming the most prolonged and expensive military endeavor undertaken by the United States between the wars in Vietnam and the Persian Gulf, with costs approaching $1 million a day.

I soon found that much of the news agenda was dictated by events in Washington. The White House was engaged in a push to get Congress on board with a steep increase in aid to El Salvador, which fed the demand for news. At first, without my own transportation, my coverage was limited to what was going on in the capital, San Salvador. Along with other members of the press, I shuttled from one press conference and embassy briefing to another, filing a steady stream of reports to CBS' hourly broadcasts. I was thrilled when I made the big drive-time radio shows for the first time: the "World News Roundup" and "The World Tonight."

I heard the Sunday homily delivered by Auxiliary Bishop Gregorio Rosa Chávez at the barren and cavernous National

Campaign advertisement, La Paz Department, El Salvador, 1984.

Interim President Alvaro Magaña (center) and alleged death-squad leader, Roberto d'Aubuison (right, in the light suit), San Salvador, El Salvador, 1983.

Cathedral. In a landmark sermon there in 1980, Archbishop Oscar Arnulfo Romero had implored the military to "stop the repression." He was shot dead days later by a sniper. Dozens of demonstrators were killed as they gathered on the cathedral steps to protest his assassination. Now, three years later, Rosa Chávez reported the weekly death toll compiled by Archdiocese's human rights office: forty-eight civilians, not counting casualties racked up in a new government army offensive in San Vicente.

I attended a press session at the baroque Presidential Palace, where a buttoned-down economist named Alvaro Magaña held forth as El Salvador's interim head of state. Magaña hadn't yet reached sixty but looked twenty years older as he burned through a pack of Benson & Hedges behind a sprawling mahogany table. The U.S. had helped broker a deal to put the more moderate Magaña in the palace, rather than Roberto d'Aubuisson, founder of the ultra-rightwing Nationalist Republican Alliance (ARENA).[1] (Investigators would later determine that d'Aubuission ordered the assassination of the Archbishop and possibly hundreds if not thousands of other political disappearances and murders.) Magaña was soft-spoken and diminutive and fielded reporters' questions with impeccable English. But rather than providing any real information, the session seemed mostly aimed at assuring American taxpayers that their investment was being well spent, that democracy was taking root in El Salvador.

That was the narrative advanced by the U.S. Embassy. Behind its thick walls and mesh screens deployed to impede the impact of rockets and grenades, glad-handing officials towed the line of a fledgling democracy "caught between extremes of right and left." In its weekly tally of violent deaths, the embassy downplayed death-squad killings linked to the security forces, chalking them up instead to "unknown forces."[2] But the extreme right was part of the government, not some faction of renegades, as our officials seemed to

believe or wanted us to believe. In the early days of the Vietnam War, embassy spokesmen had likewise treated reporters to wildly optimistic views that failed to square with discernible reality.

That same week, I got my first look at d'Aubuisson at a memorial service at the national assembly for an ARENA deputy who'd been assassinated by unknown gunmen. Family and friends emerged from armor-plated Jeep Cherokees amid a phalanx of bodyguards to pay their respects. Nearly all wore dark suits and sober faces, crossing the plaza in sweltering heat, as the military escort struck up an off-key version of Chopin's funeral march. But d'Aubuisson, lean and scrappy, sported a beige suit and broad grin, as if he just received word that a particularly irksome adversary had been eliminated. He stepped to the podium and issued a venom-laced denunciation of the perpetrators, for whom, he said, "human life has no significance or value." As I took in the scene, I couldn't help but feel I was in the company of people with ice in their veins, who had come not to mourn or reflect on the value of life, but rather to plot new ways to terminate it. D'Aubuisson had been denied the presidency—the U.S. made sure of that—but his advocacy of "total war" against the left made him a popular figure in highly polarized El Salvador, and his right-wing coalition had won enough votes in 1982 to make him head of the Asamblea Legislativa (Legislative Assembly). He put an old dentist friend of his in charge of the security detail there, and it was rumored the guards were moonlighting out of a backroom as a paramilitary force. Years later, it would come to light that the dentist, Héctor Antonio Regalado, had begun his shadowy labors during the 1970s back in his native Usulután, where he organized a local Boy Scout troop into a death squad.[3]

A malaise of menace and intrigue seemed to permeate everything in San Salvador. Perhaps most troubling was the great lengths to which people would go to act like things were normal. Unidentified assailants were dragging victims from

Fifth anniversary of the assasination of Archbishop Óscar Arnulfo Romero, San Salvador, El Salvador, 1985.

their homes in the dead of night. Their disfigured bodies would turn up days later in streets and garbage dumps. The morning tabloids invariably published news of the latest casualties—gruesome black-and-white headshots of extinguished life, together with brief, tersely worded captions. The text rarely seemed to change, other than the name and residence of the victim: "Juán Pérez, laborer, resident of Ilopango, *ultimado*—literally, finished off—by heavily armed men dressed as civilians. An investigation is underway." No more was ever said about the investigation, and in El Salvador there were tens of thousands of cases pending.

Clearly, any investigator who sought to get to the bottom of such cases stood a good chance of meeting a similar fate. Detectives just signed the death papers; they didn't *want* to know the details. Their reports were remarkably meticulous in describing the kinds of wounds, the caliber of the bullets that produced them, and from what distance the weapons were fired. Most often, it was *a quema ropa*—point-blank range. The reports were equally remarkable for their failure to identify perpetrators. It felt as though I'd entered a world of Hitchcock's creation, where black sorcery had staged a coup d'etat and where M-16s were invested with magical powers to appear at the location of their targets, aim themselves, and pull their own triggers.

Just being journalists made us suspects as well. Shortly after my arrival, one newspaper ran a full-page ad from a death squad calling itself the Secret Anti-Communist Army. The ad said that American reporters were "agents more dangerous and sympathetic to the terrorists than anyone in Moscow." I smirked at the time, but I would come to appreciate the logic behind those kinds of subliminal threats, how right those faceless people were in their twisted way, how little Moscow really had to do with El Salvador, and how much more we journalists did in terms of tipping the scales.

The Soviets may have helped arrange some arms shipments from Hanoi or Tripoli via Cuba and Nicaragua that found their way to rebel strongholds in Chalatenango or Morazán, but it was no Ho Chi Minh Trail. The evidence of a secret-arms pipeline from Nicaragua laid out in a State Department "White Paper" was flimsy and contrived.[4] Two things were certain: The Salvadoran government would not have lasted more than a few days without U.S. aid, and our reports were about the only credible counterweight to the flow of propaganda that sustained it. The newly appointed defense minister, General Carlos Eugenio Vides Casanova, told his troops that the battle for American opinion was one of the war's major fronts—"as important as San Vicente or Morazán." Journalists covering El Salvador straddled both fronts, where the war on the ground and the one back home converged. We were in its crosshairs. (Vides Casanova would be deported from the United States in 2015, after he was found liable by immigration courts for participating in torture and extrajudicial killings in El Salvador during the war.[5])

On the day after the memorial service for the assassinated politician, I visited the human-rights office of the Archdiocese. The office kept volumes of gruesome Polaroid photos of unidentified men, grotesquely mutilated, who would turn up on city streets, parking lots, garbage dumps—a catalogue of just about every variation of human perversity imaginable. Anguished women arrived throughout the morning on the back porch, often with young children hanging off their arms, and pored over the albums for clues to the whereabouts of missing husbands, sons, brothers. I noticed a neatly groomed man in his thirties was doing his best to comfort the distraught women. He introduced himself as Jacinto Morales. I asked him what he thought: Were the death squads rogue elements operating outside the military command structure, as U.S. officials maintained, or were they enmeshed in it?

He told me about three brothers who were hauled from their house one night by masked gunmen. The body of one brother was later found at El Playón, a notorious lava field that stank of rotten flesh, perpetually circled by vultures. The

Cadets at a graduation ceremony, San Salvador, El Salvador, 1983.

Protest against political killings, San Salvador, El Salvador, 1983.

other two brothers turned up in prison. "Three men captured at the same time and place," Jacinto said. "One turns up in a death-squad dump and two in the government's prison. So you tell me: Who are the death squads?"

Back on the second floor of the Camino Real, I'd park myself in front of the huge topographic map of El Salvador, 1:100,000 scale, in the CBS office. The map was covered with a clear plastic overlay smeared with red and black grease-pencil markings that showed the zones controlled by the five guerrilla armies of the Farabundo Martí, the locations of government army garrisons, rebel infiltration routes, alleged routes of arms traffickers. The map was mesmerizing, with its yellow and green contours and squiggly blue lines that suggested steep mountain hollows drained by a latticework of meandering brooks. There were countless hamlets out there in the countryside, with exotic names that fired the imagination: Anamorós, Yamabál, Cacahuatique—places where few reporters on the second floor were going to, pinned down as they often were to the capital by the news agenda. They were places where I knew I'd find the war in all its full-blown color, where the armed response to state violence had put government forces on the defensive, where there was a more level playing field, in a manner of speaking.

I'd taken a few day trips to the war zones with other journalists. But I wanted to get out there and *stay* out there. I'd I hadn't yet saved enough to get a car of my own and didn't yet have the field experience to convince CBS to finance one. I had an inkling of where I could start: the department of San Vicente. It was a picturesque region, the scene of intense combat. U.S. advisors were just launching a Vietnam-style counterinsurgency designed to seize the initiative in the countryside from the guerrillas. I could get a ride out from San Salvador and take up residence in a cheap guesthouse near the barracks where the U.S. Green Berets were billeted. It would turn out to be a perfect move.

Salvadoran Army patrol, San Pedro Hills, El Salvador, 1983.

# Ghosts of Vietnam



**I leapt into elephant grass** flattened by the helicopter's downdraft and into the war. Stooping to stay clear of the rotor blades, I sprinted for the edge of the clearing. Ten soldiers rushed past, hauling the bodies of two companions toward the chopper. Their patrol had just clashed with the rebels, I was given to understand. One soldier was dead, another wounded. They were loaded aboard, and the helicopter lifted off and banked away.

As the machine's whup-whup-whup faded into the distance, I followed on the heels of a young lieutenant named Lemus Acosta. We stalked through the stillness of the forest, the men on high alert. Acosta pressed a finger to his lips, signaling for silence. He pointed to a blood-soaked rag on the ground, then to a bush. Blood dripped from the leaves. "They've taken casualties, too," he whispered. Three or four wounded, maybe one or two of them dead, he said. We followed the trail of blood, more drops on the ground, even more on blades of grass further on. Someone had been badly hit. But the rebels soon outdistanced us, and we stopped to regroup at an abandoned farmhouse.

The helicopter ride came about on the spur of the moment. A Special Forces captain asked if I was game for jumping on a Huey that was on its way to resupply a search-and-destroy operation and evacuate casualties. And, just like that, I was dropped into the San Pedro Hills (Cerros de San Pedro) on a combat mission with one of El Salvador's newest, U.S.-trained counterinsurgency battalions.

"A decent family lived here," said Acosta, nodding toward the dilapidated house. With a trimmed goatee and Atlas-like physique, Acosta was exactly the kind of field commander that U.S. military advisors were grooming for battle in El Salvador: tough, smart, disciplined, a risk taker. He took a slug from his canteen. "About 500 people lived in the area," he said. "Now, there are only *terengos*." I hadn't heard the word before. It was military slang for "terrorists," which was how nearly every Salvadoran military commander viewed the guerrillas.

A new strategy championed by U.S. advisors called for disrupting this stretch of rugged upland jungle in the department of San Vicente. (In El Salvador and elsewhere in Central America, administrative districts are called departments, rather than states or provinces.) The San Pedro Hills constituted a strategic corridor used by the FMLN to move fighters and supplies east-west and north-south through the heart of the country. The Salvadoran Army's sudden appearance here had come as a nasty surprise. "We've forced them to split up," Acosta said. "They've been trying to regroup, but they keep running into us."

Civilians rebuilding their ravaged village, San Lorenzo, El Salvador, 1983.

Besides four years in cadet school, Acosta had received training from U.S. Special Forces officers in Panama and Colombia. Company commanders like him were in high demand, as the Pentagon moved to shape the Salvadoran Army into a force that would get out of the barracks, curtail the wanton killing of unarmed civilians, and go on offensive against guerrilla fighters in their mountain strongholds.

In the summer of 1983, San Vicente was the focal point of U.S. efforts to ramp up the war against the FMLN rebels. Broad stretches of it had fallen under guerrilla sway, and the government had been forced to abandon scores of towns and surrounding hamlets. The rebels had demolished bridges and powerlines, and a third of its population had fled the fighting and indiscriminate bombardments from government warplanes, crowding into makeshift camps in search of food and shelter or fleeing all the way to the United States.[1]

San Vicente offered a compelling landscape, both picturesque and war-ravaged. A patchwork quilt of plowed fields and bullet-pocked colonial villages were nestled along the slopes of a towering volcano. Even without a car of my own, I rightly surmised that I'd be able to get around by taxi or by bumming rides with local forces.

The lift on the helicopter came about on the spur of the moment. I had just a few minutes to race back to my room, grab some gear, and dash back to the garrison as the chopper was revving up. There were no seats, just the open deck, and I clung to any handhold I could find as we shot straight into the air, then zipped over the jungle. It amounted to an adrenaline-laced magic carpet ride, the side doors wide open, the gunners on either side studying the lush landscape below. Then, just as abruptly, a red signal flare shot up from the jungle ahead of us, and we dropped into a clearing, the pilot shouting over the roar of the engine: *¡Bájese! ¡Bájese!* Get off! Get off!

With Acosta in the lead, we slogged on through the afternoon, bushwhacking in dense undergrowth and high sawgrass. The guerrillas had vanished. By the time we reached the embattled village of Santa Clara at dusk, I was severely dehydrated. In my haste that morning, I'd forgotten to pack a canteen. Nor did I have a sleeping bag. I slung my hammock on the veranda of the town's general store, guzzled several Fantas, and shivered through the night to the yap of dogs and sporadic bursts of gunfire, nervous soldiers firing blindly into the dark.

Still, there was no place I would rather have been. The Pentagon had chosen San Vicente to launch a Vietnam-style counterinsurgency campaign, replete with a fresh infusion of Huey UH-1H helicopters, C-47 "Puff the Magic Dragon" gunships, mortars, howitzers, and more M-16s than the Salvadoran Army had recruits to handle. A dozen Green Berets, all veterans of Vietnam, were training "hunter" battalions and pushing them out into the jungle on search-and-destroy missions. The advisors had also initiated a "hearts and minds" pacification campaign to "steal the banner of the left," implementing a series of modest reforms—plots to small farmers, $1 a day to townsfolk rebuilding their shattered villages—to give rural families a taste of something more than the terror and poverty that had been their daily bread for the past half-century of military dictatorship. It didn't seem to matter that the strategy had failed in Vietnam. They were convinced that the social landscape was different in El Salvador, that here it could succeed.

I took up quarters in a cheap hotel just off the main square of the departmental capital. The barren room was perfect for my purposes. There was a twin bed and a table and chair to work at. I wrote at night by candlelight during the frequent outages occasioned by rebel sabotage to the power grid. A floor-to-ceiling window opened on to a small balcony that overlooked the palm-fringed square, dominated by an old, wedding-cake-style clock tower. As nighttime advanced and the wind rustled the palms and carried the prattle of gunfire in from the distance, I had the sense of living in the pages of a Graham Greene novel.

The hotel was a few blocks from the local branch of Antel, the state telecommunications company, where I went each morning to file my latest dispatches to CBS. I would place a collect call to the radio desk in New York, unscrew the mouthpiece of the phone to hook my alligator clips into the line, then send off the pieces I had written up and tracked overnight. From Antel, it was a short walk to the Salvadoran Army's 5th Brigade barracks, a crenellated fortress where the Green Berets were billeted. Luckily, they were under orders to accommodate the press, and I was one of just a few foreign journalists staying in town. The Pentagon needed the American public—and Congress—to get behind the war effort and its growing price tag. I took advantage.

Most accommodating of the officers all was a sandy-haired Special Forces captain from Minnesota named Jeff Nelson. "Just don't use my name," he said the first time we met. It was Nelson who'd gotten me on that helicopter to the San Pedro Hills. A few mornings later, I hopped in his jeep for a ride to the shooting range outside town. Recruits popped off rounds at paper silhouette targets under Nelson's gaze and wriggled under bursts of live-round fire.

The captain had been involved in secret missions in Vietnam and Cambodia during the 1960s, but he didn't want to talk much about it. He bristled when I asked how that experience compared with his work as an advisor in El Salvador. "We don't use that word—advisor," he said. "It conjures up ghosts." Ghosts of creeping involvement in a prolonged, unpopular, and unwinnable guerrilla war. The preferred terminology was "trainer." That was because, he said, "You guys impact our ability to function." Journalists were supposed to play along with the fiction, even though officers were seen with combat weapons in places where they weren't supposed to be, doing their best to go incognito. I'd spotted one myself, his white face concealed by layers of camouflage paint, ears stuffed beneath the flaps of a fatigue cap. He did his best to avoid me, but I managed to squeeze off a frame of him glowering at me as he disembarked with troops from the back of a transport truck and gunfire popped down the road.

One sunny afternoon, Nelson took me halfway up the slopes of the San Vicente volcano to Guadalupe, a bullet-pocked village of cobblestone streets guarded by steely-eyed paramilitaries. In frontline towns like Guadalupe, Nelson and his colleagues were scrambling to reform the notoriously abusive rural civil defense patrols. The patrols were originally formed during the 1960s as part of President John F. Kennedy's Alliance for Progress to serve as a bulwark against Castro-inspired revolution in the countryside. But they'd far exceeded their mission, rounding up and summarily executing suspected rebel sympathizers, often on little evidence.[2] Critics asserted that their excessive zeal had created even more guerrillas in response to the campaign of terror. They had since been disbanded, but now the Green Berets sought to clean them up and put them back on the firing line. They were seen as too valuable an asset to the U.S.'s counterinsurgency strategy.

The patrols would be responsible for fending off guerrilla attacks on static targets, like towns, bridges, and transmission towers, freeing the hunter battalions to go on the offensive. The advisors also hoped to broaden the recruitment base of the patrols to include less ideologically fervent volunteers, to get them off the fence and join the fight against the guerrillas. "You want to polarize the situation," one advisor said of the expanding civil defense effort. It wasn't clear to me that further polarization was what El Salvador needed by the Summer of 1983.

Fifty men gathered on the village's football pitch for the day's training. Nelson himself was barred from giving the lecture, since the patrolmen were technically part of the security forces, not the military. He stood to the side while a Salvadoran officer exhorted the group to refrain from torture and summary execution and to generally respect human rights. It was hard to know what, if anything, stuck in the heads of the blank faces assembled before us.

Salvadoran Army recruits (left) and funeral procession (right), San Vicente, El Salvador, 1983.

Nelson beckoned me to join him for an open-air ride in the bed of a pickup truck for the ride back to town. I asked the captain if he wasn't simply helping to reconstitute a Frankenstein that would once again prey on fellow townsfolk. "First of all," he said, "these guys know if they abuse the people, the guerrillas will execute them first chance they get." I was startled by his honesty—this frank acknowledgment that America's putative enemy served as the most effective deterrent to government abuse in rural communities across El Salvador. Maybe that was how many Salvadorans saw them, too. Maybe that was why they'd been able to persist and replenish their ranks, even as the U.S.-backed war effort intensified.

But for American officials and their Salvadoran counterparts, the solution was a military one—to vanquish the rebels outright on the field of battle.[3] That meant more money, more weapons, more death. "We could win this war if the United States would just give us the support we need," Acosta complained to me that evening in Santa Clara. The people in Congress, he told me, were holding up the show. "They think the subversives are fighting us with arrows," he said. "Let me tell you, they have everything—RPGs (rocket-propelled grenades), hand grenades, M-16s, G-3s. The only thing they don't have are airplanes."

The counterinsurgency campaign was bound to produce more casualties—especially among junior officers like Lemus Acosta. The top U.S. advisor said as much a few months later at one of his weekly press briefings at the U.S. Embassy in San Salvador. "The life expectancy of a lieutenant under fire is very low," Colonel Joseph Stringham told us. A Vietnam veteran of unconventional warfare, Stringham was head of the U.S. Military Group, as the contingent of fifty-five Special Forces advisors in-country was called. In keeping with the policy to downplay America's growing role in the war, we were invariably reminded at the briefing's outset of the ground rules: We could identify Stringham as a "Western observer or a military observer but not both."

Ghosts of Vietnam indeed. Even as it pumped more aid and more guns into tiny El Salvador, the Pentagon tiptoed around the effort, trying to reassure the public back home that it wasn't really our war. We were keeping our footprint light. We'd put up the money, the weapons, the training; the Salvadorans would shed the blood. It was "still a low-level, low-intensity, light-infantry war," Stringham said. With astonishing candor, he added: "It's still little brown men fighting little brown men."

Salvadoran Army soldiers, Las Marías, El Salvador, 1984.

Indigenous Civil Defense patrol Todos Santos Cuchumatán, Guatemala, 1983.

# THREE

# The Invisible War

**Western Highlands, Guatemala,
August 1983**

**A gaunt figure stepped from the shadows** and thrust an old bolt-action rifle toward my chest. A handwoven poncho hung from the man's boney frame; a straw hat was cocked on his head. From beneath the hat's brim, I could make out classic Mayan features—straight, jet-black hair, high cheekbones, a Romanesque nose. "What are you doing out here?" he demanded. "Don't you know it's after curfew?" A half-dozen more men, similarly dressed, armed with vintage carbines, emerged from the darkness and pressed in around us.

We were in Uspantán, a dreary town of dusty streets and low-slung, cement-block buildings in Guatemala's Western Highlands. It was late August 1983, and I had come to Guatemala with French journalist Edith Coron to get a firsthand look at a largely invisible war. A brutal counter-insurgency campaign was underway across northwestern Guatemala, but little of it was being reported in the U.S. The military was said to have razed hundreds of Indigenous villages in its efforts to root a leftist insurgency that had taken hold among the native Maya population. Reports indicated that thousands, perhaps tens of thousands, of villagers had perished at the hands of the Guatemalan Army just in the past eighteen months.

The conflict was unfolding in a region of rushing rivers and steep mountain slopes. There were few roads, and access was made even more difficult by checkpoints and travel restrictions that discouraged outsiders from nosing around. Moreover, unlike El Salvador, U.S. military assistance was not pouring into Guatemala, which had been ruled by a succession of brutal military dictatorships and figurehead presidents since the Central Intelligence Agency (CIA) overthrew a democratically elected leftist government in 1954. So abysmal was Guatemala's human-rights record that, in 1977, the Carter Administration imposed a ban on military aid, and it remained in effect. The restriction of aid meant there was less demand for news back home and less pressure on Guatemala to open the war fronts to the press. That state of affairs had pretty much given the Guatemalan military carte blanche to conduct a no-holds-barred campaign against the guerrillas and their suspected supporters among the Indigenous Maya.[1] The Reagan Administration was seeking to overturn the ban; the President himself asserted that Guatemala was getting a "bum rap" on human rights.[2]

In tandem with the extreme violence, the military had launched a program of *auto-defense patrols* throughout the Altiplano of western Guatemala. The patrols were not unlike the Civil Defense in El Salvador, in the sense that they acted like a "force-multiplier," that freed the army to conduct offensive operations rather than simply guard static targets.

But, as I would find out, in Guatemala they served a larger counterinsurgency purpose: to impose strict control over the Indigenous Maya, who accounted for more than forty percent of the country's population.

We'd seen similar patrols earlier in the day on our way north from Guatemala City. We came upon a roadblock, the first of many, about four hours after departing the capital. A group of fidgety Mayan patrolmen waved us to a halt before a makeshift gate. Like the men here in Uspantán, they were dressed in grimy, handsewn garb, and they brandished a mishmash of old shotguns and carbines. They scoured our rental car—the glove compartment, under the seats, the trunk. Where were we coming from? Where were we going? What was our business? Finally, they hoisted the gate and let us pass but not before taking down the license plate number. There was no doubt our presence would be reported immediately to the nearest garrison.

In Uspantán, the patrolmen insisted on taking us directly to the local commander. I'd heard several stories that concluded unhappily for those summoned before military authorities. In one particularly harrowing episode, the army had rounded up nine men in Uspantán itself. They were handed shotguns and made to dress in uniforms to look like guerrillas. Then they were taken by helicopter to a road outside the village of Chajul, some thirty miles away, where the army then staged an ambush that killed them all. Their bodies were left by the roadside and served as a pretext for the army to launch a door-to-door campaign of searches, abductions, and terror.[3]

Of course, we enjoyed a layer of protection unavailable to the average campesino. Not that the military had any great love for reporters. For starters, the Guatemalan government refused to issue press credentials to journalists. That alone served to put us on notice: Our safety could not be guaranteed. Nearly sixty Guatemalan journalists had met violent deaths or had disappeared in the past three years alone. None of the perpetrators had been brought to justice. We nonetheless received a cordial welcome from Uspantán's commanding officer, a mustachioed young lieutenant named Otto Recinos who beckoned us to sit. He wasn't so gracious with our Indigenous escorts.

"We think they have small brains, a limited ability to think," Recinos said. He nodded toward the patrolmen as they filed out the door. He didn't seem to care whether they heard him or not. It was the Indigenous Maya's failure to grasp the rudiments of civilization, he asserted, that lay at the root of Guatemala's peasant rebellion. "What has been the cause of the subversion?" Recinos mused. "I'll tell you, it's not just here in Guatemala. It's the same as with your *negros* in the United States. Here, our problem is with the *indígenas.*"

But surely, I asked, the good lieutenant made allowances for the abuse and violence the Indians had endured for centuries. Might that not account for their attraction, however misguided, to notions of land reform and social justice? Recinos fixed me with a quizzical look, as though he suspected I might sympathize with the heathen. "When they get sick, they prefer to go to their 'witch doctors' instead of seeing a real doctor," he said. "Give them a bed to sleep on, they'll smash it up for firewood and sleep on the floor."

Recinos was himself a *ladino,* mestizo, which placed him several rungs above the Indigenous villagers on the ladder of Guatemala's highly stratified social hierarchy that reached its pinnacle with a small elite of European stock. As if to underscore the racial dimensions of the conflict, someone had scrawled in fading letters on a wall we'd passed on the street: *Ladino visto, ladino muerto*—Ladino seen, ladino killed. With fresh paint, the military offered a rejoinder at the entrance to the command post: *Guerrillero visto, guerrillero muerto.* In this war of ideas, it seemed the army had gained the upper hand.

Where were we going from Uspantán? Recinos asked. To Nebaj and points beyond, I told him. He'd recently been assigned there, he said, but he didn't elaborate on the nature of his mission. The village of Nebaj served as gateway to the

Indigenous Civil Defense patrol, Huehuetenango Department, Guatemala, 1983.

Guatemalan Army troops, Ixil Region, Guatemala, 1983.

"Ixil Region," a culturally rich area of about 300 square miles, named for the Mayan subgroup that inhabited its slopes and hollows. The region was delineated by Nebaj, together with Chajul, and the village of San Juan Cotzal, separated from one another by dirt roads that wound through the mountains. Ixil. The very name evoked a kind of mystical resonance. *EE-sheel*. It was partly the legendary Indigenous culture, the beauty of its lush green landscapes, and the vibrant textiles woven and worn by its people. But it was also in part because of the resistance that had arisen within its rugged folds, marking it as ground-zero in the war that would determine the fate of Guatemala.

"*Buena suerte*," said Recinos with an ominous tone. "Say hello to Nebaj for me." He went to the door and barked into the darkness: *¡Patrulla!* Soon, an escort of five men materialized to see us to our guesthouse.

We arrived in Nebaj on a cold and rainy morning two days later. Green hills rose just beyond the main street, which had been churned to a muddy soup by exhaust-belching military trucks. Women huddled under the eaves of the whitewashed adobe buildings that lined the thoroughfare, swaddling infants in handwoven *huipiles* patterned in bright reds, greens and yellows, the colors of the Indigenous Nebaj. Several sat on their haunches just outside the doorway of the army's impromptu field headquarters. I wondered if they might be widows so desperate for assistance they would seek it from the very same men who killed their husbands or sons.

In a dimly lit room inside, Lieutenant Colonel Mario Aquino Flores treated us to an impromptu briefing. "The Ixil Triangle is the region most affected by Marxist-Leninist subversion in all of Guatemala," he began, using the military's preferred name for the region. The subversives had "deceived" the Ixil with promises of land, food, and paradise. Citing Mao Zedong's famous analogy, Aquino likened local support for the guerrillas to a sea in which fish swim—the fish being the guerrillas. The comparison was certainly apt when it came to Mao's communist guerrilla forces in rural China a half-century earlier. But Aquino Flores turned the Chairman's adage on its head: The Guatemalan Army, he declared, was now "draining the sea," leaving the rebels high and dry and gasping for air.[4]

The army's strategy was two-pronged, Aquino Flores explained, summed up in a simple alliterative slogan: *fusiles y frijoles*—"rifles and beans." On the one hand, the government was obliterating the rebels' base of support through brute force. It was putting rifles, even if they were antiquated carbines and shotguns, into the hands of Indigenous villagers who had previously sided with the guerrillas, forcing them to take the army's side. On the other, the army was spearheading a rural development scheme to feed the thousands who had survived the violence and were returning home only to find scorched crops and smoldering ruins. The high command was directing the reconstruction effort, which involved concentrating the Maya in "model villages" designed to exercise full control over their movements and activities. The idea, Aquino Flores said, was to undercut any chance for the rebels to regain their former strength. Civilians who remained in the mountains and refused to submit to military control were regarded as enemies of the state. Commanders called them "illegal communities" and treated them accordingly. They lived a life on the run, scavenging anything they could find for survival, hounded by infantry sweeps, and subjected to frequent artillery bombardments.[5]

A rickety watchtower loomed ahead of us at a bend in the road. It looked like a relic from the Wild West, as though Fort Apache had been magically plunked down amid the electric-green hills of Guatemala. The tower straddled the entrance to the model village of Río Azul, an Indigenous Maya community that was in the process of rebuilding. Villagers scurried about, lugging planks and hoisting zinc roofing to the top of newly built clapboard houses. Surveyors pounded stakes as they laid out future streets along an orderly, geometrical grid.

A handsome man in his early thirties offered to show us around. His name was Nicolás Rivera Chávez, and he was the head of Río Azul's civil defense patrol. The entire community had fled when fighting broke out in early 1982. "It was too dangerous to stay," he said, shielding his eyes against the late-afternoon sunlight. They'd returned just a few months ago, after the army declared the zone "cleansed of subversives." The traditional community had been made up of tidy adobe homes surrounded by small garden plots, joined together by footpaths that wound through the hills. But when they returned, they found everything in ruins. "All the old houses were burned down, our corn fields destroyed," Rivera said. Did he have any idea who the culprits were? "Who knows?" he shrugged. "Armed men who move through the mountains." I took note of the deliberate vagueness. It was as honest a response as he could muster—and still be safe. Soldiers were within earshot; Rivera had to choose his words carefully.

The army was dictating the terms of Río Azul's resettlement. Everyone was required to live within the confines of the model village. No more scattered houses backing up on to the woods, where guerrillas could find refuge, treat their wounded, and stock up on supplies and intel. Like elsewhere in the Western Highlands, all men were obliged to join *la patrulla civil,* Rivera said. A handful of his patrolmen milled about nearby under the vigilant gaze of a soldier. They carried the same M-1s and battered shotguns that seemed to be the hallmark of Indigenous civil defense patrols everywhere. "We suspect some of the índios may still be with the subversives," Recinos had told me back in Uspantán. They weren't to be trusted with the army's standard-issue weapon—the Israeli-made Galil assault rifle. Even so, community leaders were required to keep a meticulous inventory of their armories, noting which guns were checked out to whom at the start of a shift and making sure all were returned at the end of it.

To my mind, the weapons seemed more symbolic than anything else. The idea was to get the Maya to renounce their former guerrilla friends in the most absolute way possible—by brandishing arms against them. Whether the *patrulleros* actually fired them in combat was almost beside the point. There was something else about the patrols that was far more important, and it had little to do with the guns. It was what the obligatory service did to the minds of the men who were forced to join. It imposed a Machiavellian form of social control over the Indigenous peasantry, shattering the bonds of community that had defined village life since time immemorial. Patrol members were expected to report on their neighbors, even on each other, if anything seemed amiss. It amounted to a vast spy network. Everyone was a suspect, everyone a potential informant. Fear and suspicion ruled the day.[6]

The army was also doing its best to push its version of Guatemala's recent history. Whatever violence the Maya had suffered, they had only themselves and their friends in the Marxist subversion to blame. It was the ultimate gaslight: If the army had responded with brutality, commanders told the Maya, it was only to save them from an even worse fate.

Dissent of any kind could prove highly prejudicial, if the interviews I conducted by roadsides and market stalls were any indication. When soldiers were nearby, the story was always the same: "We returned to find our neighbors dead and our home in ruins. We don't know who did it." But whenever I questioned people beyond the reach of eavesdropping ears, their accounts were very different. It was the soldiers, they whispered. They'd seen it with their own eyes: troops in uniform torching homes and fields, shooting anyone who tried to run.

We followed a network of backroads across the frontier into Mexico. At the end of a winding tire track, we came upon an encampment of a few dozen shelters cobbled together from scraps of timber and plastic sheeting. A small crowd of refugees gathered. "When the army comes, they kill the

Sister and brother at a corner shop, San Juan Cotzal, Guatemala, 1983.

Indigenous children in a food line, Nebaj, Guatemala, 1983.

people and burn our homes," said a gaunt man in his 50s. He said he'd witnessed soldiers gunning down neighbors, setting houses and fields ablaze. I listened intently, allowing the tape machine to record his words. I could detect no trace of anything rehearsed, staged, or disingenuous. How did he know it was the army? I asked. "One knows," he said to nods of agreement. "Who else has helicopters and trucks?"

I told them what military commanders had said to me, that they wanted refugees to return to Guatemala, that no harm would come to them. "They'll kill us as soon as we get to the border," said a wide-eyed man in a voice that wavered with terror. "Besides, what would we go back to? Our village is gone. There's fear everywhere. We've been through too much to go back."

Nearly three decades later, the coup of 1954 engineered by the CIA at the behest of the United Fruit Company continued to reverberate. Had the U.S. allowed Guatemalan democracy to flourish, it's unlikely there ever would have been an armed resistance. It's unlikely that Guatemala would have had a military dictatorship so repugnant that the parent who birthed it ended up disowning it. The coup also radicalized the political left, stimulating revolutionary guerrilla movements throughout Latin America. The lessons seemed especially resonant in neighboring El Salvador and Nicaragua, feeding a conviction that social change could only come about through the barrel of a gun.

By the time the Guatemalan Civil War came to an end in 1996, 200,000 people had perished, half of them in the decade of the 1980s. The United Nations Truth Commission appointed to investigate human-rights abuses found that eighty-three percent of the victims were Indigenous Maya and seventeen percent were Ladino. More than 600 massacres had been committed, nearly all by the military, the commission concluded, and 420 villages had been razed. The army, security forces, and related paramilitary groups were responsible for ninety-three percent of all human-rights abuses and acts of violence the Truth Commission was able to document.[7] Another 42,000 civilians were reported to have "disappeared," meaning they were abducted by security forces, likely tortured for information and eventually killed, their bodies made to vanish in unmarked graves or thrown from "death flights" over the ocean.[8] As the civil war continued into the 1990s, a declassified cable from the CIA station in Guatemala reported:

> The well-documented belief by the army that the entire Ixil Indian population is [pro-guerrilla] has created a situation in which the army can be expected to give no quarter to combatants and non-combatants alike.[9]

Declassified cable traffic between U.S. Embassy officials in Guatemala and the State Department in Washington would later provide a clear indication of tacit U.S. support for the bloodletting from the early months of the Reagan Administration. "If…the GOG [government of Guatemala] can successfully 'go it alone' in its policy of repression, there is no need for the U.S. to provide the GOG with *redundant* [emphasis added] political and military support," wrote one State Department official in a memo to Washington in October 1981.[10]

Back at the Embassy in Guatemala City, spokesman Martin Ronan provided a hint of that support when he told us upon our return from the Western Highlands that "most accounts of massacres are either not true or exaggerated."

FMLN guerrilla fighters, La Anchila, El Salvador, 1983.

# FOUR

# Meet the Rebels



**T**he scene resembled a well-crafted movie set, as the men ambled toward us, single file down the cobblestone street. Some wore jeans and plaid shirts, others were dressed in ill-fitting olive fatigues and baseball caps. All were armed with weapons of war— a mix of M-16s, West German G-3s, a Belgian FAL. They strode past bullet-pocked adobe walls of fading blue and pink pastels, dappled in bright scarlet graffiti: *¡Revolución o Muerte! Long live the FMLN! Death to the Death Squads!*

These moments, when we approached armed strangers, were fraught with tension and potential danger. You never knew exactly how things would unfold. By now I'd encountered the FMLN rebels in other places, beginning with an encounter in the ghost town of Tenancingo with photographer Bob Nickelsberg of *Time*. I studied the way Bob and other, more experienced journalists handled themselves, and I did as they said: at checkpoints, when drawing near combatants of one side or another, or when gauging the right time to leave before things went sideways. I was developing a sense of how to act, what to ask, when it was cool to break out my camera or pull out my microphone to document the moment. I'd noticed in dealings with both sides that the rebels, the very people the U.S. was paying to exterminate, were the

more welcoming to the press. Still, even if a meeting was nonthreatening, there was always the chance that a warplane might suddenly appear overhead or that an ambush could be lying in wait in no-man's land on the way out.

A grizzled-looking veteran with an M-1 rifle slung on his shoulder descended the hill on an aging, clip-clopping mare. Graying hair sprouted wildly from beneath a cap jammed backwards on his head. An intricate pattern of crow's feet surrounded his deep-set eyes. I judged him to be in his mid-fifties. He yanked on the reigns and brought his mount to a halt. "Who does this asshole Reagan think we are?" he shouted as our camera rolled. "Doesn't he understand we're not going to surrender? We're in this war to the finish!"

It was October 1983, and I had led CBS correspondent Richard Wagner and a film crew to the picturesque town of San Agustín in the war-ravaged department of Usulután. Wagner had just arrived from New York to do a story about the Reagan Administration's latest efforts to bring the rebels to heel, promoting a program that offered amnesty if they turned in their weapons and joined the "democratic process." White House special envoy Richard Stone was on his way to Central America to promote the plan, but it was really aimed at the American public and Congress. The rebels would not disarm without some ironclad guarantees for their safety, like a concomitant dismantling of the security forces, and the White House knew it. They had been there before, and their followers had been slaughtered. No matter. The idea was to make the guerrillas seem obstructionist, unreasonable, undemocratic, thus paving the way for increased military aid to break them on the battlefield.

The man on horseback said he came from San Francisco Javier, the next town over, and he had been an activist with the centrist Christian Democrats for twenty years. But two years ago, he joined the guerrillas after seeing the military steal one election after another and gun down his fellow party members when they tried to protest. "They started killing our people," he said. "There was no choice but to grab a rifle, civilians against the government." His horse reared impatiently. "We don't always know what the directorate is thinking," he continued, referring to the leadership of the FMLN. "But there's one thing all of us here agree on: They'll have to kill us all before we surrender. It's either victory or death."

It might have sounded like a canned bravado, had it come from one of the adolescents moving down the street on foot. But the wizened elder had an arresting, unvarnished presence, and his words seemed to encapsulate why so many men and women had chosen to take up arms in this tiny country— and why it was proving so difficult to vanquish them.

Despite mounting infusions of U.S. aid, the rebels of the Farabundo Martí were on a sustained offensive in the Fall of 1983, routing government forces across the entire eastern half of the country. Dozens of cities and towns had come under attack. Army and civil defense units were pulling back from dozens more. In some locations, government soldiers were surrendering en masse, together with their weapons. Lots of U.S.-supplied armaments were finding their way into rebel hands. I was uniquely positioned to witness these events. In September, just as the offensive began, I convinced CBS to finance my purchase of a used 1977 Mitsubishi Colt Lancer. With the mobility afforded by that car, I made myself the network's eyes and ears in the backcountry, filing for CBS Radio and scouting stories for visiting correspondents like Wagner.

I had also begun filing stories with accompanying photographs for Cox Newspapers and the chain's flagship, *The Atlanta Journal-Constitution.* Recording audio, making photographs, and taking notes, I was gathering evidence, trying to create as a truthful account as I could of what I was witnessing to share with faraway audiences who nonetheless had a say in what happened on the ground here in places like Usulután.

In the company of other journalists and sometimes on my own, I learned the ropes. I came to know which towns were ruled by jack-booted paramilitaries, where I was likely to find a guerrilla patrol, and which hamlets lived in a kind of perpetual twilight zone—where neither the government nor the rebels had the strength to maintain a permanent presence and villagers had mastered the art of befriending both sides without unduly arousing the suspicions of either. I gained a sense of when it was relatively safe to venture up one road, when an ambush might lay in wait down another. I developed an ear for when someone was telling the truth and when someone was telling me what he or she thought I wanted to hear.

The department of Usulután lay just across the Lempa River from San Vicente. With a watershed that drained nearly half the country on its way to the Pacific, the Lempa was El Salvador's principal waterway. It was spanned by two main bridges, both leading from San Vicente into Usulután. Guerrilla sappers had blown up the Puente de Oro on the Coastal Highway in late 1981, and they would later do the same to the Maximiliano Hernández Martínez Bridge on the Pan-American Highway. Their sagging cables and dynamited midsections put you on notice as you crossed their hastily erected prefab replacements that you were entering a land where government control was tenuous and everything was up for grabs.

The volcanic slopes of its interior to the north were cool, forested, pleasant. But Usulután's coastal plain was a sweltering cauldron of DDT-laced cottonfields and cañaverales, bisected by backroads lined with nasty, mud-walled ranchos.

Salvadoran Army roadblock, Usulután Department, El Salvador, 1984.

In the days and nights following the destruction of the Puente de Oro, the Salvadoran Army conducted a campaign of terror in reprisal through the Lower Lempa. Hundreds of civilians in several Usulután townships were said to have been rounded up and executed, likely producing even more recruits for the rebels among the survivors.[1] The "depth of the insurgency" in Usulután, one U.S. officer told me, was such that trying to extirpate the rebels from their mountain strongholds in Chalatenango and Morazán would be a "piece of cake" by comparison to efforts that would be required here. It was a department up in arms, flush with combat-hardened guerrillas supported, at least tacitly, by broad swathes of the local population.

The department seemed to offer a surprise at every turn. One day on the Coastal Highway, I came upon a rebel road-block just four miles east of the departmental capital. The guerrillas had pulled a loaded bus to the side of the road. I followed two rebels up the stairs of the bus: one of them going row to row collecting *impuestos de guerra*—"war taxes"—from passengers while the other delivered a blistering harangue against the government. He warned that the FMLN might soon respond to the army's draft with a recruitment drive of its own. Worried mothers cast sidelong glances at the teenagers sitting beside them. It was just a warning. A collective sigh was palpable when the pair hopped off the bus taking only the taxes, but no recruits, with them.

Late one afternoon with Edith Coron, I turned off the same highway where a sign pointed down a dirt road toward Jucuarán. Top U.S. advisor Colonel Stringham had told reporters that coastal Jucuarán on the Pacific had become a principal entry point for clandestine arms shipments smuggled in from Nicaragua aboard fishing trawlers. Our curiosity aroused, we started down the road. Within a few miles, we came to the banks of a wide river. The bridge across it had been dynamited, its twisted steel wreckage lying half-submerged in the current. Clearly, we weren't going any further.

And then, in the mysterious golden glow of the late-afternoon sunlight, we made out a cable-guided raft approaching from the far side of the river. To my astonishment, a dozen men bearing rifles were on board.

As they drew closer, we could see they were dressed in a ragtag assortment of jeans, fatigue shirts, and ball caps. Guerrillas. A slender man in his mid-twenties stepped off the barge first and introduced himself as the squad leader, named "Ernesto." He had brownish hair, he was clean-shaven, and an Israeli-made, folding-stock Galil was slung across his shoulder. The rifles were a common sight in Guatemala, where Israel had stepped in to assist the military when U.S. support was suspended. But it was rare to see one here. He said he had stripped off a dead army officer. His men belonged to the Rafael Arce Zablah Brigade (BRAZ), a crack guerrilla unit of 1,000 fighters that had been spearheading the fall offensive throughout the east. "The army loses territory and casualties to us every day," Ernesto boasted. "But what can you expect from an army of crap officers leading soldiers they've press-ganged into service? They have no idea what they're fighting for."

What would it take for us to go all the way to Jucuarán? I asked. I was thinking it would be great to come back with a crew to do a television piece. Ernesto said we'd be welcome but that it would be too long a trek to the town with cumbersome TV gear. He suggested it would be possible to float a vehicle across on the raft, then drive the rest of the way. "From there," he said, pointing to the far embankment, "the road is clear all the way to the center of Jucuarán."

A week later, I returned with CBS driver Nelson Ayala, *Evening News* correspondent Mike O'Connor, and a camera crew. With the help of local campesinos, we pushed Nelson's Ford van up a pair of sagging planks and on to the raft. They poled us across to the other side. We spent two more hours bouncing in third gear along a cobblestone thoroughfare, our eyes trained on the sky in hopes we wouldn't be spotted

FMLN guerrillas, Perquín, El Salvador, 1984.

Crossing the Río Grande de San Miguel,
El Salvador, 1983.

Interview with a rebel commander,
La Anchila, El Salvador, 1983.

and strafed by a government warplane. It was a relief when we finally pulled into the colonial village of Jucuarán, where a detachment of fighters marched back and forth on the dusty square to the bark of a drill instructor.

I noticed a striking-looking man who was locked in animated conversation with a fighter on the edge of the square. He had long sideburns and bushy eyebrows, and he kept pushing a whisp of thinning blonde hair off his forehead. It turned out to be the revolutionary, Belgian-born priest Rogelio Ponseele (sometimes spelled Poncell.) Seldom glimpsed by journalists, Ponseele had fled San Salvador after death squads eliminated several of his parishioners and bombed his church at the start of the war. For the past three years, he'd been ministering to guerrillas and their peasant supporters in the mountains of Morazán. Conservatives in the bitterly divided Catholic Church believed clerics should steer clear of politics. But other priests like Ponseele had embraced liberation theology, prioritizing social justice and the "preferential option for the poor." Some practitioners believed it was just to take up arms to defend against oppression.

Though he'd chosen a life on the run with the guerrillas, Ponseele said he also made a conscious choice not to bear arms himself. "I've never fired a shot," he told me. "I want them to understand that I am with them to share the Gospel and to bring people together in peace." As he spoke, I raised my camera and snapped a rare frame of him on the battlefront. He was one of the most famous guerrillas in the country—and certainly one of its most wanted. Radical clerics like him were seen by the military as dangerous instigators who had helped the FMLN make to deep inroads among the poor and persecuted in devoutly Catholic El Salvador.

Later that evening, we were introduced to the presiding commander. His nome de guerre was "Cirilo," and in a tight-fitting t-shirt and a beret cocked atop his head, he sported the look of a classic guerrilla comandante. He smirked at the notion that boatloads of weapons were arriving from Nicaragua on the beaches down the hill from town. There was no need, he said. The United States itself, by sending guns to the army, was arming his fighters. Just in the past month, Cirilo claimed, the Zablah Brigade had killed 400 soldiers, wounded hundreds more, and stripped them of hundreds of weapons—rifles, mortars, machineguns. "The advisors think that more aid is the answer to defeating us," he said. "They are mistaken in their analysis." He patted his M-16 and added: "But, anyway, we thank Mr. Reagan for the help."

Of course, even if they had been bringing in weapons from Nicaragua, as the U.S. alleged, the FMLN rebels would never have admitted to it. Even so, their claims of capturing much of their weaponry from government forces had the ring of truth. Not only because they were overrunning army garrisons and armories, but because of historical antecedents. In the early days of the Vietnam War, when American military personnel were still playing an advisory role to the South Vietnamese army as they now were in El Salvador, the Viet Cong guerrillas captured thousands of the firearms from our Vietnamese allies.[2] We ended up, in effect, arming our adversary. There was good reason to believe the U.S. was doing so again.

Survivors of a massacre, Chalatenango Department, El Salvador, 1984.

# FIVE

# Gualsinga River



I **eventually found a small apartment** in posh El Escalón, a bastion of the rich and powerful that overlooked downtown San Salvador. Its steeply sloping streets were lined with middle-class homes interspersed among the walled compounds of coffee barons, factory owners, generals, and government ministers. They were impenetrable fortresses, topped with floodlights and razor wire—the last lines of defense in a joint-venture of public and private capital and American aid that stretched all the way out to the search-and-destroy units combing the hills of Morazán for guerrillas of the Farabundo Martí and their peasant supporters.

My place was a converted garage adjoining my landlady's modest, single-story home. The old garage was probably the most exposed, insecure dwelling in the entire district. Its louvered glass windows looked across the street at a thirty-foot-high wall that featured gun slits and peep slots through which the eyes of security guards studied my comings and goings. I never met the neighbors who lived behind those fortifications. They entered and exited through a steel gate in a bullet-proof Jeep Cherokee with smoked windows, attended by a small army of men in aviator sunglasses and polyester suits bulging with weaponry.

Getting to know the neighbors was no easy feat in El Escalón. I had no idea that an academic lived on my block until Maria, my housekeeper, told me a professor two doors down had been found dead that morning, slumped over his desk. I did hear the report of a gun in the night, the punctuated, deliberate shots that betrayed chilling intentionality. Apparently to make sure no witnesses were left behind, his live-in maid and gardener had also been executed.

Without a garage, I had no choice but to park my car on the street, which, of course, subjected it to open scrutiny. One day when she arrived at the apartment, Maria told me neighbors were asking where I was going with that car: Why was it always splattered with mud around the wheel wells and sideboards? "I have no idea," she said in voice of mock innocence, recounting how she feigned ignorance. "I would never tell them anything, don Scott," she said in a whisper. "They don't have goodness in their hearts."

I wondered if I might fall prey to a new "denounce-a-subversive" hotline advertised on the radio to encourage listeners to phone in anonymous tips on suspicious activities. I stopped using a typewriter at night. The clattering of keys could easily be heard on the street outside. Someone might wonder what I was writing, or *why* I was writing at all. I started scrawling notes by hand. Even then I strained my ears with every rustle of the bushes outside, every scamper of an iguana across the roof, every car that slowed to a crawl at the corner stop sign. Death squads were still on the loose, no one had been brought to justice, and home could be the least-safe place of all. It was unlikely they would target a gringo journalist, but it couldn't be discounted completely. The sense of paranoia was infectious. Those more immediate noises that signaled potential peril often announced themselves against a low, distant rumble like thunder on the wind. U.S.-supplied Dragonfly jets were dumping their payloads on Guazapa, a volcanic massif just twenty miles to the north where the rebels maintained a permanent presence, fleeing in advance of ground assaults or sheltering in tunnels from aerial attacks.

By now I'd met the guerrillas on many occasions across central and eastern El Salvador—mostly chance encounters in the twilight-zone towns or, by now, even larger cities where they were vying with the government for control and influence. But I hadn't yet ventured into their "liberated territories" where they had established a parallel revolutionary government with its own systems of health care, education, justice, and communal labor. As many as 200,000 peasants still lived in the areas under rebel control by the fourth year of the war. It was a remarkable number, considering the torment they endured from sustained bombardments and army sweeps. Salvadoran military commanders were near-unanimous in their contempt for the *masas,* or "masses," as the rebels' supporters were called, and few officers had qualms about targeting them on operations.

That would come into sharp relief when we received a tip at the CBS office in early September 1984 that the army's crack Atlacatl Battalion may have committed a massacre in the northern department of Chalatenango. The region was a stronghold of the Popular Liberation Forces, or FPL, one of the five rebel armies of the FMLN. News of the alleged atrocity was so fresh that the guerrillas hadn't yet announced it on their clandestine radio programming. Reuters correspondent Bobby Block and I raced to the Jesuit-run Central American University, where we received instructions from a well-connected priest on the route we should take and how we could bluff our way past army roadblocks to get there. The military would not want journalists covering such a story; reporters had been killed for far less. But we'd have to get moving. By midmorning the next day, the priest surmised, they would choke off any possible routes of access to the zone. The padre also said he would send word to the rebels to expect us. I had no idea how he would do that, and I didn't ask.

At first light the next day, we set off with CBS camera crew Roberto Pineda and Jaime Robles in Nelson's four-wheel-drive Land Cruiser. Just as the priest predicted, the soldiers manning the last checkpoint in Chalatenango were on the final hour of their overnight shift. The new shift would almost certainly bring orders to seal off the road. Evidently, such orders had not yet been received. They checked our IDs, eyed the TV gear. Where were we going and for what? We explained that we were filming a documentary about the nuns who ran an orphanage in the next town up the road. They mulled that over as I passed around a pack of smokes. "When are you planning to return?" the squad leader wanted to know. I guided the flame from my lighter to the tip of his Marlboro. Tomorrow or the day after, I said. He nodded with a touch of gravitas, exhaled a cloud of smoke. Then he ordered his men to let us pass. We'd made it through.

It was nearly dark before we entered the hamlet of El Zapotal. To throw the army off, we'd taken a roundabout route to get there. Rebels were swarming everywhere, loading huge gunny sacks on to a train of horses and mules, about to set out into the mountains. We presented our press cards to a scruffy young man who said he was the officer in charge. We told him we wanted an armed escort to the site of the massacre on the Gualsinga River. He said we'd have to wait, took our credentials, and vanished down the street.

We slung our hammocks on the veranda of the town store. Night was falling fast, and the sky broke open in driving torrents. Just as we were about to turn in, a dark figure in a

Rebel fighter with an armadillo, Chalatenango Department, El Salvador, 1984.

wide-brimmed hat dashed in from the downpour, an old M-1 in hand. Permission had been granted, he said. We would leave at daybreak with an officer and fifteen *muchachos*— young fighters in training, assigned to protect civilians in the FMLN's rearguard.

Bobby pulled out his shortwave radio and tuned it to Radio Farabundo Martí, the clandestine news and propaganda program of the FPL, the second-largest of the five rebel armies of the FMLN. The broadcaster announced the "Gualsinga River Massacre" and proceeded to reel off the names of thirty-nine victims, with ages ranging from late seventies to a month-old infant. "We call on (President) Duarte to bring to trial the murderers of the Atlacatl, which is nothing more than death squad disguised as an elite battalion," the voice said. The Atlacatl was the U.S.-trained, elite battalion that had been commanded by Lieutenant Colonel Domingo Monterrosa, the darling of American advisors for his take-charge aggressiveness. But a shadow trailed Monterrosa and the battalion. He and his men stood accused of butchering 1,000 civilians—mostly women, children, and elderly—in a hamlet called El Mozote in the rebel stronghold of Morazán in 1981. More recently, the Atlacatl was alleged to have executed as many as 100 civilians in strife-torn Cabañas Department.

The perpetrators of such deeds were rarely held to account. Whenever reports of government atrocities surfaced, Salvadoran commanders understood that evoking the specter of a Marxist victory was sure to keep U.S. aid flowing and shield their own from punitive action.[1] Tropical conditions also conspired to favor the executioners: bodies decomposed quickly, making allegations easy to deny and equally difficult to prove. The broadcast was the rebels' first public acknowledgment of the Gualsinga incident. We'd made it into the rebels' *territorio libre* just before the door slammed shut; no one else would make it in. We'd still have to deal with getting out, but we couldn't think about that now.

The morning light revealed our location on a high ridge, overlooking a misty valley of fluorescent-green jungle. Mountain peaks stretched back as far as the eye could see. The leader of our patrol, a dark man with unruly black curls and scraggly beard named "Chevo," pointed to a range far off in the distance. "That's where we're headed," he said. "Maybe we'll get there tomorrow." The rest of our escorts were all young kids. One of them, a slight fifteen-year-old named Miguel, seemed to have a permanent, ear-to-ear smile. He looked like an eager Little Leaguer, wearing a ball cap several sizes too big. Only Chevo and another guerrilla had M-16s. The rest were armed with vintage M-1s.

We proceeded single file along a mountain path, pushing on through intermittent rain. Toward the late afternoon, we could hear the faint rush of distant water, getting louder as we walked. I emerged from dense undergrowth to behold a wide, rain-swollen stampede of water. Entire trees were being swept downstream in a brown, swirling rush. We were perched atop a sheer cliff thirty feet above the water. "The Sumpul River," Chevo announced. "We'll have to cross here." The Sumpul was the scene of one of the war's deadliest massacres in 1980, when Salvadoran and Honduran army troops and helicopter gunships trapped and killed at least 300 civilians, many of them drowning as they tried to flee.[2]

Before us, a dilapidated footbridge sagged across the river. It was in such a state of disrepair that the footboards out in the midsection dangled off a single wire, perpendicular to the water below. We'd have to cross one at a time, hand-over-hand, clinging to a single guidewire and stepping on the ends of the boards. To avoid vertigo and panic, the Salvadorans advised us not to look down at the raging torrent. I handed my camera bag to the ever-cheerful Miguel, who danced across the bridge. My crossing was far less graceful. We'd still have to come back this way, but the journey by now had acquired an insistent logic that propelled us forward, with little regard for how we would retrace our steps.

Resting after crossing the Sumpul River, El Salvador, 1984.

Twilight was falling when we reached a ramshackle hut. After a dinner of beans and tortillas, we fell fast asleep in our hammocks. By midmorning the next day, we were descending a soggy path toward the Gualsinga when the nauseating, sickly smell of death filled the air. Five badly decomposed bodies were strewn across the footpath, still draped in rotting scraps of clothing. I reached down with a stick to lift a woman's gingham dress. To my horror, I discovered a backbone and rib cage still inside. A baby bottle bobbed in a rank puddle alongside two shattered skulls. I retrieved a tiny cranium the size of an infant's and found a bullet hole cleanly drilled through the back.

"This was an entire family, murdered in cold blood as they tried to get away," said Chevo. He led us further down the path toward the rush of the Gualsinga. The woods were strewn with a patchwork of clothes of all colors and description. It looked like the scene of a plane crash. A child's pink knapsack hung from a branch. A full scalp of long, black hair lay amid a pile of clothing. A human stampede ran along the path, Chevo said, people ditching the last of their belongings as they raced toward the riverbank.

We backtracked and soon came upon an elderly couple and a gaggle of half-naked children. They were just returning home in the aftermath of the attack. An emaciated old man named Julio Cartagena huddled alongside his wife, Dolores, on a pile of boards outside their house.

Mortar shells began to crash all around them on the night of August 28th, they said, just as they were putting their children to sleep. Cartagena, sixty-one, said he barely had time to strap on his small rucksack, where he kept a few meager essentials and family documents for just such an eventuality. The Cartagena family and some 300 peasants fled for their lives, accompanied by a small escort of FPL militia.

For two days, army soldiers stalked them through cornfields, across mountain brooks, down steep mountain paths. On the third day, the panic-stricken peasants found themselves hemmed in against the Gualsinga River when helicopters dropped fresh troops behind them to block their escape. On previous incursions by government forces, Cartagena said, he and his family and neighbors had been able to flee the assault and eventually escape. But never had they experienced the bewilderment and terror that accompanied the sudden appearance of helicopters on the hilltops to their rear. Surrounded and physically drained, the peasants huddled in silence through the night to await their fate. The next morning, the army moved in. The rebel detachment directed the people down the path toward the river. There was nowhere else to go. Gunfire erupted. Some of the peasants were cut down then and there. Others flung themselves into the Gualsinga's rushing waters.[3]

"A soldier tried to grab me," Cartagena said. "I thought, 'My God, they're going to kill me.'" But the soldier only managed to pull off his backpack. He plunged into the Gualsinga. The current swept him far downstream. Miraculously, the children and Dolores also managed to wash ashore. Many others were dragged down by the icy current and drowned.

Neighbors gathered around, eager to speak. Amid the breathless recollections, we struggled to sift fact from hearsay, trying to nail down what people actually saw as opposed to what others had told them. It was clear the testimonies were spontaneous and unrehearsed. It couldn't have been otherwise, for most of the people were just emerging from hiding. Up the lane came a fragile-looking, barefoot young man. He looked like a medieval waif, with oversize rags hanging off his pencil-thin frame. His name was Jesús. He didn't know his age, but I guessed he might be around twenty. "I took flight and crawled into a hole for shelter, like a dove who builds a nest," Jesús said with disarming naivete. From his hiding place, he witnessed troops butcher two girls "with those knives they have on their rifles."

A man named Pascual Ayala said he'd lost his entire family. "I had a small child with me when I dove in the water,

Mourners, Santa Cruz Loma, El Salvador, 1985.

Guerrilla couple on New Year's Day, Tenancingo, El Salvador, 1985.

Rebel graffiti, Chalatenango Department, El Salvador, 1984.

but I couldn't hang on," he said vacantly. "The older girl came behind me, but the current was too strong." The two daughters drowned. His wife and two other children were shot dead by the soldiers. I consulted the list I'd jotted down two nights before from the Radio Martí broadcast. Sure enough, five Ayalas were on it, including a one-month-old infant and a seven-year-old girl. I was at a loss for words.

In its plan to "take the war to the guerrillas," the U.S. had stepped up the delivery of Hueys to the Salvadoran military in recent months, more than doubling the size of its helicopter fleet in the course of 1984.[4] The choppers enabled the army to hopscotch deep into the FMLN's mountain redoubts, dropping troops behind rebel lines to launch surprise assaults and to forcibly "evacuate" civilians from rebel-held territory. Some fifty noncombatants were rounded up and taken away in the helicopters, compounding the bewilderment and grief of the survivors.

"It looks like they want to eliminate all of us, so that there are only people like them left," Dolores Cartagena said. Like everyone we met in the hollows and ravines of Chalatenango, she called the guerrillas "our army," and she referred to the government army as "the enemy."

Tens of thousands of noncombatants had already been driven from zones controlled by the FMLN in a sustained bombing campaign over the previous two years.[5] As in the days of the Vietnam War, U.S. officials cited the flight of civilians to displaced-persons camps, now housing a tenth of the country's population, as evidence that support for the government was on the rise. While giving a major boost to offensive operations, the helicopters also offered potential for capturing or eliminating the most recalcitrant civilian *masas* who hadn't already fled, delivering a severe blow to rebel logistics and morale. I was beginning to think that we had just witnessed the results of a trial run of that strategy.

Getting back to San Salvador proved almost as tricky as getting in. To hide evidence of our trek, we shaved before leaving El Zapotal. We scrubbed the mud off our pants and boots, put on fresh shirts. We stashed videotapes and film beneath the spare tire. Months earlier, a television crew's materials had been confiscated by the army following a visit to rebel-held Chalatenango. In 1982, four Dutch journalists were ambushed and killed by government soldiers as they attempted to rendezvous with guerrillas, also in Chalatenango.[6] At an army roadblock, we were subjected to close questioning. Our vehicle was thoroughly searched, but the soldiers didn't check beneath the spare. Our cover story held up, and we were allowed to proceed.

CBS News executives in New York decided that our videos of the skeletal remains, the piles of discarded clothing, and the on-camera interviews were inconclusive. They chose not to broadcast the story. President José Napoleón Duarte conceded that a tragedy had occurred on the banks of the Gualsinga. But he claimed it was the rebels' fault; they'd used the *masas* as "human shields," he said. The Archbishop's office in San Salvador reported that fifty civilians had been killed, of which thirty-one bodies had been positively identified. The U.S. Embassy did not send anyone to investigate, but officials at the U.S. Embassy invariably downplayed allegations of army atrocities committed in rebel territory, claiming the *masas* were "not exactly innocent civilians." Elliott Abrams, Assistant Secretary of State for Human Rights, denied point-blank that a massacre had occurred.[7] Often such denials were enough to get Stateside editors to back off the story. To its credit, *The Atlanta Journal-Constitution* ran my account on the front page.

Elite soldiers of the Sandinista Popular Army, Jinotega Department, Nicaragua, 1985.

# SIX

# The Element of Surprise



**T**he **U.S. was conducting** a different sort of proxy war in Nicaragua, directing an insurgency aimed at overthrowing the Sandinista government. By 1984, the counterrevolutionary rebels, known as the "Contras," were wreaking havoc in the interior of Nicaragua. The Contras' campaign largely consisted of sabotage, roadside ambushes, attacks on thinly-defended farming cooperatives, and targeted assassinations of government officials—all aimed at undermining the Sandinistas' morale and their program of radical social and economic transformation.[1] Despite the obfuscations and dissembling regarding the role and objectives of the Contras, it was becoming increasingly clear that the Reagan Administration had deployed the CIA in a full-fledged effort to overthrow the Sandinistas, to make them "say uncle," as President Reagan himself would eventually concede.[2] With the eye of the Central America storm shifting toward the escalating conflict in Nicaragua, I made my first trip there in the Spring of 1984 and eventually moved there in 1985.

Entering Managua at the end of an all-day drive, I was struck by its wild exuberance and unruliness. How utterly different it was from San Salvador's oppressive, morgue-like atmosphere. A decade after Managua had been flattened in an earthquake, its downtown still lay in shambles. Squatters occupied the skeletal hulks of four- and five-story buildings, rooms on the upper floors exposed to view where their walls had fallen away. Unmown grass overflowed medians along the boulevards. Yet everywhere young people crowded the roadsides, shouting, laughing, flashing peace signs, push-starting disabled vehicles. (A U.S.-imposed trade embargo made spare parts scarce.) They hitchhiked in large groups, pulling one another aboard the beds of rolling dump trucks, hanging off their running boards.

Certainly, support for the revolution was far from unanimous. There were landowners who'd lost properties to confiscations, others who were harassed by the police or detained by State Security, suspected of supporting the counterrevolution. Owners of independent media feared censorship or potential shutdown. Ordinary citizens were struggling to make ends meet. The war and the trade embargo, compounded by the Sandinistas' own mismanagement, were pushing the economy toward free fall. Price controls and rationing had spawned a thriving black market, and inflation was spiraling. But the people had rid themselves of a tyrant and were trying to forge a new future. Driving that first time through the streets of Managua, I couldn't escape the impression that I was witnessing something extraordinary—an infectious, irrepressible, and spontaneous outburst of optimism and national pride. This tiny country was standing up to the Yankee Colossus. The *joie de vivre* itself seemed like a collective act of defiance. Even the unruly vegetation seemed to wave a banner of insurrection.

American journalist Bill Gentile and his Nicaraguan girl-friend, Claudia Baca, graciously offered to put me up in their tidy, single-story home in a residential section of Managua. I soon found my way around town and familiarized myself with the lay of the land. As I got to know Nicaraguan families and was invited into their homes, I got the sense that support for the Sandinistas was quite strong and intergenerational. It wasn't just kids rebelling against parents. In many households, kids, parents, and even grandparents appeared to be on board with the revolution's goal of creating a more equitable society.

President Reagan's characterization of Nicaragua as a "totalitarian dungeon"[3] was so at odds with reality as to be laughable, had it not been for the bloodletting that accompanied the rhetoric. But then, deception was woven into the very fabric of his Nicaragua policy. In the early days of his tenure in 1981, Reagan authorized the CIA to reconstitute the despised National Guard of the former Somoza dictatorship into a guerrilla army—the Contras. Their purported aim was to interdict alleged arms shipments from the Sandinistas to the FMLN guerrillas in El Salvador. It made for a complex situation—with the U.S. supporting guerrillas in Nicaragua while seeking to vanquish guerrillas in El Salvador. It tested the ability of journalists who covered both conflicts to communicate with clarity to audiences back home. In some ways, the countries were mirror opposites. In both instances, the Reagan White House claimed that vital national-security concerns were at stake.

In fact, the Contras never interdicted anything. The claims of weapons shipments to El Salvador from Nicaragua were wildly exaggerated from the start, calling to mind the overblown incident in the Gulf of Tonkin that served as pretext for full-scale U.S. intervention in Vietnam two decades earlier.[4] The Contras were intended for an altogether different purpose:

to wreak havoc inside Nicaragua and bring the Sandinistas to their knees.[5] The entire effort was built on a lie, and other lies followed. The Contras supposedly operated from bases within Nicaraguan territory. But their camps were really located across the border in Honduras.[6] U.S. and Honduran officials on the receiving end of American largesse sought to maintain this fiction. Reporters played along to assure continued access, fudging the location of their stories with the deliberately vague dateline: "On the Honduras-Nicaragua Border."[7]

My first visit to Nicaragua coincided with a CIA-orchestrated attack on the Pacific port of Corinto that was intended to look like a Contra operation.[8] In echoes from twenty years earlier when sea-borne Filipino and Chinese operatives were hired to raid coastal installations in North Vietnam, the Agency organized third-country Latino mercenaries to mine Nicaragua's main harbor from highspeed "piranha" boats, launched from a "mothership" in open waters.[9] I joined an entourage of journalists on a tour organized by the Sandinista Defense Ministry aboard a fishing boat jerry-rigged with a boom that was supposed to detonate mines before they struck its hull and sank the vessel. A lighthearted air attended the event, with plenty of jokes about the clumsiness of the attempted deception. The International Court of Justice in The Hague later found the U.S. in violation of international law for mining the port and more broadly for "training, arming, equipping, financing and supplying" the Contras as well as for encouraging the Contras to engage in "acts contrary to general principles of humanitarian law."[10]

Unlike El Salvador, where the war was everywhere, finding the conflict in Nicaragua required a more concerted effort. It took several hours by car north from Managua, across scrubby tablelands and then up through mist-shrouded forests and coffee groves, to reach the lonely dirt-track roads that led to the theater of war. I joined Gentile, who at the time was stringing for NBC Radio and making photographs for United Press International (UPI), for my

Contras burning a Sandinista newspaper, Quilalí, Nicaragua, 1987.

first jaunt into the northern mountains. The thoroughfare seemed to offer an ideal perch for ambush at every turn, and the roadside was littered with the burned-out hulks of East German transport trucks and white Toyota pickup trucks that had fallen victim to Contra attacks. The Toyotas, Gentile explained, were the vehicle of choice for civilian personnel of all sorts—schoolteachers, engineers, agronomists. To fend off Contra ambushes, they had taken to arming themselves, blurring the line between what constituted a military and a civilian target. "Traveling in one of those things is like playing Russian roulette," said Gentile said as we passed the wreckage of a Toyota pickup. "Then again, pretty much any vehicle is fair game as far as the Contras are concerned. Even ours."

On a road winding road in northern Nueva Segovia Department, we encountered a Sandinista militia unit spread out along the crest of a hill. From the early days of the war, the revolution's defense relied on hastily organized, ragtag units like this one, drawn mostly from local farm hands. There were both men and women in their ranks, and as we came upon them, they were lining up for a lunch of chicken and rice scoped out of twenty-gallon pots from the back of a UAZ jeep. The *milicianos* were outfitted with Makarov pistols, AK-47s, and a smattering of rocket-propelled grenades, and they sported a slapdash assortment of olive-green caps and ochre-colored field shirts. It's hard to say what would have happened if the neo-conservatives in the U.S. administration hadn't bent everything they saw in Central America through the prism of the Cold War. But for the Sandinistas, the lessons of the Guatemalan coup continued to resonate three decades later: obtain weapons from wherever and whomever will provide them. Even if that seemed to confirm Washington's suspicions that they were acting at the behest of America's archrival—the U.S.S.R.

The morale of the Sandinista militia members seemed to be holding, even as they found themselves increasingly outgunned and outmaneuvered by Contras infiltrating from Honduras. Still, several said they were willing to lay down their lives to build a more just and egalitarian society. "I'm ready to stay out here for as long as the revolution dictates," said one volunteer who called himself Fredy. But beneath the bravado, darker thoughts seemed to lurk. When I asked him for his last name, Fredy demurred. He feared reprisal, he said. Evidently, not everyone in this corner of the backwoods shared his enthusiasm for the Sandinista program.

Contra ranks were swelling. Thousands of peasants had been rounded up by Contra raiding parties and herded back to the base camps in Honduras for training before reentering Nicaragua as rebel fighters. But large numbers also went voluntarily. Some had family ties to other recruits, others had become disaffected with government efforts to collectivize farmland or impose price controls on the fruits of their labor.[11] The Sandinistas unfailingly called them mercenaries, butchers, and "*la guardia*"—the ex-National Guard of the Somoza dictatorship. Whatever may have motivated their fighters to join, the Contras had come to be seen by the comandantes in Managua as an existential threat to the revolution that required a commensurate response: a national mobilization.

The ensuing commandery draft included not just peasant kids from the war zones, but tens of thousands of educated, middle-class youth from the cities on the Pacific coastal plain. With a resulting influx of draftees, the Sandinista Popular Army (EPS), went about forming a series of elite Irregular Warfare Battalions (BLIs), similar to units U.S. advisors had helped forge in El Salvador. As the number of BLIs grew, the Sandinistas began to deploy them in multi-battalion pincer operations designed to encircle and hammer the Contras.

In May 1985, I once again joined Bill Gentile, now a *Newsweek* photographer, on a foray into the mountains to witness the evolution of the war. In just a year's time, it had become increasingly difficult to access the backroads leading to *las frentes de guerra*. They were mostly sealed off by Sandinista checkpoints, and it could take some guile to get

Aftermath of a Contra ambush, Santo Tomás, Nicaragua, 1987.

Funeral procession for a fallen leader,
Managua, Nicaragua, 1984.

Sandinista Popular Army convoy,
Jinotega Department, Nicaragua, 1987.

past. Such was the case when we started up a road deep in the mountains of Jinotega Department and presented a safe-conduct letter from the Defense Ministry to a pair of young soldiers. The letter was meant for another unit, in a different location. But with some easy banter, we cajoled them into letting us pass, and suddenly there we were, cut loose in the combat zone.

We followed the road as it snaked deeper into the mountains, our eyes glued to the blind turns ahead for a possible ambush. We emerged hours later on the floor of a wide valley, where a huge convoy of military transport trucks was pulled off on the roadside, engines idling. It turned out to be the entire Santos López BLI, and one of its commanding officers, Lieutenant Noel Talavera, recognized Gentile. The battalion was on its way into combat, he said, and he invited us to come along as the convoy rumbled north toward the hamlet of El Cuá.

Two mornings later, the trucks disgorged half the battalion on to a grassy hilltop. Talavera and his deputy, a Chilean exile who went by the name "Rogelio," led us into a valley of patchy forest and dew-drenched fields. As the sun cleared the ridge behind us, we could make out a farmhouse perched on a distant bluff. Smoke curled from its chimney. Through his binoculars, Talavera made out a lone figure moving around the yard. We re-entered the forest and soon came upon a grove of coffee bushes sagging under the weight of unpicked beans—red, swollen, rotting. "Look at this shit," Talavera muttered. "Total fucking waste."

The Contras had been waging a campaign to sabotage the coffee harvest, Nicaraguan's most important earner of foreign exchange. To help bring in the harvest across the war zones, the Sandinistas recruited tens of thousands of *brigadistas*, including office workers, students, and foreigner volunteers. They were handed rifles and given cursory training to fend off Contra attacks. It was a dangerous undertaking: Two hundred brigade members would end up dying during the 1985 harvest alone.[12]

We entered the farmyard just as a gaunt, bearded man exited an outbuilding, bucket in hand. His name was José Gutierrez. He said he hadn't seen the Contras lately. *La guardia,* he called them, showing his disdain for Contras or at least wanting to create that impression. What about his coffee, Talavera asked skeptically, why had he left it to rot? "They told us not to cut it," said Gutierrez. He lived there with his wife and children for the past five years, when the government had expropriated a large estate and handed out parcels to area families, including his own. "We figured it was best to leave the coffee on the bush," Gutierrez said. "Better to lose the harvest than risk them burning everything you own." His wife, a burly woman with a thick mane of black hair, came out to check on the commotion. Several children, grimy-faced and wide-eyed, took refuge in the folds of her skirt. "You know," Gutierrez went on, "he who has the guns makes the rules."

It was clear who'd been making the rules around here, and it wasn't the Sandinistas. Despite his battalion's formidable numbers and firepower, Talavera couldn't claim to be doing more than just passing through. Nonetheless, he told Gutierrez, his battalion's presence signaled a definitive shift. "Those sons of whores are on the run now," Talavera said. "We're going to kill as many of them as we can and push the rest back to Honduras."

The Sandinistas had been gaining the upper hand recently, thanks, ironically, to lessons from Vietnam they were applying with some skill to their own counterinsurgency program. Earlier in 1985, they'd begun to forcibly relocate thousands of farming families from rural areas to create "free-fire zones" that allowed the Sandinistas to bring heavy artillery and attack helicopters to bear on broad swaths of the countryside while reducing the risk of civilian casualties. Unlike El Salvador or Guatemala, where government forces deprived guerrillas of their civilian bases of support by far more indiscriminate means, the Sandinistas rounded up peasants and transported them to fortified farms they called

Dead Contra, Cerro El Saíno, Nicaragua, 1985.

"auto-defense cooperatives." The Contras suddenly found themselves bereft of the foodstuffs, information, and recruit base they'd come to depend on. The tactic of free-fire zones was pioneered by the U.S. in Vietnam, but its effectiveness there had been undermined by an overzealous application of aerial attacks beyond the designated districts. Those attacks produced staggering numbers of refugees, who resented the loss of their livelihoods and the forced separation from their ancestral lands.[13] The Sandinistas were more restrained. It could be said that they were better at counterinsurgency.

As if to keep his word to the farmer, Talavera directed a surprise assault that evening on a Contra encampment. Just as we reached another farm late in the afternoon, advance scouts detected the group of Contras atop a hill directly across the valley from our own position, about three or four hundred yards away in a straight shot. As twilight spread across the land, the Contras went about setting up camp, even using flashlights, oblivious to our presence. At Talavera's signal, the Sandinistas commenced the attack. Red tracer rounds zipped out into the blackness like Roman candles. The valley reverberated with cracks, thumps, and concussed echoes from the machinegun fire, mortars, rockets, and grenades launched at mountainside across the way.

The pursuit resumed at dawn. Picking our way up the hill, we came upon a grotesquely contorted body clothed in a greenish-blue field shirt—standard CIA-issue for the Contras. Talavera kicked the body over. "Someone, search this guy's pockets." The troops fanned out as we continued uphill. "They don't stand and fight like they did two or three years ago," Talavera said of the Contras. "They thought they were going to take Jinotega and Matagalpa and then go all the way to Managua. Now, they're *hecho mierda*—completely fucked."

Just then, a series of shots rang out, followed by a burst, then another. "I got the bastard!" a soldier shouted. More gunfire erupted. Deliberate, single shots. Another wounded Contra, apparently left to fend for himself by his fleeing comrades, sniped from the brush. A loud crackle from an AK followed. "Surrender, you motherfucker!" He would not. More shooting ensued. More voices joined the chorus: "Give up, asshole! We've got you surrounded!" Still more gunshots popped. "Got him!" a soldier shouted from the thicket. And that was the end of it.

The Contra's body was dragged into the clearing, his pockets searched. Soldiers came in one by one, depositing captured gear at Talavera's feet. Pouches of ammo, three rifles, hand grenades. Attesting to their hasty retreat, the Contras also left behind hammocks, tents, ponchos, canteens. All issued by the U.S. Army. As Talavera reported the results to his C.O. on the radio, the mountains reverberated with the distant thud of mortars and bleating of a heavy machine gun. The Contras were coming under fire from another battalion in the next valley over. Here on this hilltop, the attack had produced four kills, no more. Still, as Talavera barked the after-action report into the handset, he said: "We've killed fifteen *guardia*." Clearly, Washington had not cornered the market on half-truths and disinformation.

I was left wondering about something else: If the Contras were simply mercenaries, like the Sandinistas insisted, why had those wounded rebels fought to the finish? Were they were so committed to their cause that they'd fight to the finish? Or had their commanders convinced them they'd suffer a fate worse than death if they surrendered?

The events added one more piece to the broader mosaic I was always in the process of constructing and rearranging in my mind. Firsthand experience was the only way to distinguish between information and its opposite. Amid the claims and counterclaims, that ever-changing mosaic was the only thing I could count on to steer me toward an approximation of the truth. I strove to bear in mind that my understanding was tentative: At any turn it could be thrown in a new direction if the next piece in the mental jigsaw puzzle didn't quite fit where I expected it to.

Miskito villagers, Haulover, Nicaragua, 1985.

# SEVEN

# The Miskito Coast

**Yulu, Nicaragua,
November 1986**

**A** caravan of ten shiny Toyota pickup trucks careened past as I headed from the airport into the center of Puerto Cabezas, the Atlantic Coast port of lofty palms and clapboard shacks that served as the region's seat of government. The Toyotas were standard transport for government and FSLN officials. But these trucks were packed with long-haired Indigenous warriors, fully uniformed and armed. I was dumbstruck. I'd met with small groups of anti-government Miskito rebels on previous trips to the Miskito Coast. But now, nearly eighty fighters were piling out of the trucks in front of the government's regional headquarters.

Clearly, the cease-fire the Sandinistas first extended to Miskito rebels in 1985 was now being embraced by another contingent of the fractious Indian movement. I could tell right away that these fighters were new to the peace process: Their brand-new, U.S. Army-issue uniforms and fresh, out-of-the-crate weapons said it all. They must have been allied to the main Contra army, the Fuerza Democrática Nicaragüense (FDN), until very recently. The same camouflage fatigues were beginning to turn up elsewhere on Nicaragua's frontlines. I'd seen Contra commanders wearing them in Nueva Segovia, and, in Jinotega, Sandinista officers had begun sport-

ing them as war trophies, recovered from dead or captured Contras. But the gear and guns on display in Puerto Cabezas evidently had been airdropped to fighters no longer willing to put them to their intended use.

The Miskito and two smaller Indigenous groups, the Sumo and Rama, joined the war against the Sandinista Front in late 1981. From the outset, the CIA and Pentagon sought to fold the Indigenous struggle into their strategic designs to overthrow the Sandinistas. The Atlantic Coast was an Achilles heel for the Sandinistas; it was remote, difficult to reach. The culture was also distinct, historically more oriented toward Kingston and Miami than Managua.[1] Fearing the Contras and their U.S. backers would try to stake out territory and establish a provisional government there, the Sandinistas overreacted, to put it mildly. They torched villages, machine-gunned cattle, forcibly relocated communities. Entire villages fled north into Honduras, filling refugee camps that provided recruiting and operational bases for the Miskito guerrillas.[2] The Indigenous army that emerged from the Honduran camps, called MISURA, allied itself closely with the FDN. Another Indigenous guerrilla force, MISURASATA, grew out of coastal communities further south and based itself out of Costa Rica. Its rank and file were more removed and more skeptical of the FDN and its CIA overlords. As their leader, Brooklyn Rivera, put it: "The CIA cowboys want us to be their little Indians."[3]

By the mid-1980s, this schism helped the Sandinistas woo disparate bands of Miskito rebels from the bush. The government allowed the rebels to keep their weapons and promised them limited self-rule. The region's isolation and the shifting loyalties of its Indigenous fighters made the Miskito War a wildcard in the larger struggle over Nicaragua's fate. And despite the scant coverage of events and its status as a sideshow to the main event, the Miskito War held important strategic implications for the wider conflict between the FSLN and the Contras.

President Reagan's hyperbole about them being the "moral equivalent of our Founding Fathers" notwithstanding, the White House always had trouble selling the Contras to the American public. Their command structure was dominated by former National Guard officers of the odious Somoza dictatorship, and their human-rights record was abysmal. The Indigenous insurgents, on the other hand, provided a propaganda punch the rest of the Contras lacked. The Reagan Administration's professed concern for Miskito rights never found similar expression when it came to the genocide in Guatemala or to the U.S.'s treatment of its own Indigenous people, for that matter. But at the conclusion of a five-hour "fact-finding" mission to Managua, Republican Congressman and Reagan loyalist Bob Dornan barked into my microphone that the Sandinistas were "genocidin' the Indians." And Reagan himself, mimicking President Kennedy's *Ich bin ein Berliner* speech from 1963, proclaimed during a visit to West Germany twenty-two years later: "I am . . .a Miskito Indian."[4]

In truth, if the Contra leadership had promised the Miskito guerrillas half of what the Sandinistas ended up offering them and had the U.S. been willing to acknowledge their aspirations for autonomy, the revolutionary government in Managua would have faced far greater peril. But taking the Miskito people seriously would have meant placing issues of Indigenous land rights and self-governance on the Nicaraguan agenda, far more than could have been hoped

for from those driven by Cold War anti-communism in Washington. Perhaps taking the Miskito, Rama, and Sumo on their own terms was more than could have been expected from any dominant "Western" culture, including that of the Sandinistas. But crucial policy errors committed by their adversaries gave the Sandinistas badly needed time to repair damage and learn something from their mistakes.[5]

The reversal of allegiances began in 1985 in the Miskito village of Yulu, about an hour's drive inland from Puerto Cabezas. It happened to be around the same time as Reagan's speech in Germany. An initial group of sixty guerrillas approached the government troops under a white flag, directly contravening orders from their commanders, who believed that negotiating with the Sandino-communists was tantamount to treason. So, without wishing it, the Miskito rebels who shook hands on a ceasefire became the foes of their old comrades in arms.

In addition to my other reporting duties, I started working for *Newsweek* that same year, just as I began covering the Miskito War. In September 1985, I attended a raucous assembly of 700 Indigenous delegates in the steamy jungle outpost of Rus Rus, Honduras, just to the north of the Nicaraguan border. Organizers hoped the assembly would bring order and unity to the flagging Indigenous insurgency. But the gathering soon devolved into shouting, finger-pointing, and recriminations. At that meeting a pair of mysterious gringos who claimed to be "Canadian pilots" seemed to direct the proceedings from behind the scenes. One of the "Canadians" told me that the CIA and FDN had lost confidence in the Miskitos' willingness to fight. "Nobody will take them seriously until they get their act together and unify," he said. "That's what this thing is all about." He and his shadowy colleague encouraged the delegates to endorse the old leadership's hardline position, in league with the Contras and the U.S., to press for regime change in Managua. The conference produced a new political-military organization, KISAN, a Miskito acronym for

Miskito rebel leader Uriel Vanegas (left with raised hand) and Sandinista Comandante and Interior Minister Tomás Borge (right), Puerto Cabezas, Nicaragua, 1987.

Miskito fishermen, Haulover, Nicaragua, 1985.

Nicaraguan Coast Indian Unity. But dissenters said the group was new in name only and that those open to a negotiated end to the conflict with the Sandinistas were shunted aside.[6]

A few weeks later, I had the rare privilege of visiting Miskito communities along the Nicaraguan coast, traveling by outboard-powered dugout canoe with Uruguayan photographer Daniel Caselli and an Indigenous interpreter. Wherever we came ashore at a coastal hamlet, a barefoot boy would quickly shimmy up a palm tree and knock a few coconuts to the ground. An adult would then whack them open with the deft swipe of a machete and hand them to us to drink. There was a lot of warmth and humanity in that simple gesture. In the picturesque community of Haulover, wedged on a neck of land between the Atlantic and a sapphire-blue lagoon beneath a row of lofty coco palms, villagers watched as a contingent of Sandinista soldiers dismantled an earthen bomb shelter, honoring a request from residents to remove the fortifications. Haulover had been the site of three major clashes between Miskito insurgents and the Sandinistas, most recently just a few months earlier. Tensions were beginning to ease, but villagers said they still wanted the government troops to leave.[8]

Hearing that I had attended the Rus Rus gathering, they invited me that night to report on what I had seen and heard there. I felt like a medieval town crier as I fielded questions to a full house in the village's Moravian church, the interpreter translating my responses from Spanish to Miskito. Standing before the crowd, I felt the full weight of my responsibility to recount the events as accurately, thoroughly, and impartially as  possible, culling from memory who said what and when, in minute detail. When we shoved off into the surf in our dugout the next day, the entire village turned out to wave goodbye.

I returned to the Miskito Coast in November 1986 with Bill Gentile. We'd gotten special permits that authorized us to make the trip overland from Managua, following one of the most dangerous roads in the entire hemisphere at the time: hundreds of miles of single-lane, washed-out tire tracks through desolate, rebel-infested jungle and savannah. Except in the environs of the besieged mining towns of Siuna and Rosita, we encountered no other traffic the entire way.

Our journey had taken on extra urgency as tensions mounted in Nicaragua. Congress had just approved $100 million in fresh aid to the Contras, and the rebels were gearing up for a major new offensive. American warships loaded with Tomahawk missiles were cruising the waters off Nicaragua's Atlantic Coast. With the influx of aid, pressure was on to get the Contras out of their camps in Honduras and into Nicaragua. A Contra invasion of the northern Atlantic Coast had long been contemplated in Washington, and it was said to be under consideration again.[7] It was the Sandinistas' most vulnerable flank, far removed from Managua, inhabited by Indigenous and Creole communities that regarded the Sandinista revolution with indifference and, in some cases, outright hostility.

But the Iran-Contra scandal was also beginning to unfold in Washington. Vice Admiral John Poindexter had resigned as National Security Advisor. Lieutenant Colonel Oliver North had been sacked from the National Security Council. The startling revelations—that Poindexter and North conspired to sell arms to Iran in exchange for Western hostages taken in Lebanon, then diverted the proceeds to the Contras—had sapped much of the Reagan Administration's strength in Washington. Credible allegations were beginning to surface that the Contras were also raising money while a congressional ban on assisting them was in place by trafficking drugs to the U.S. aboard the same aircraft that North had contracted to secretly parachute guns to them inside Nicaragua.[9] With officials from the President on down scrambling for cover, a U.S.-backed Contra invasion seemed less likely than it had just a month earlier. Still, rumors persisted that an invasion scheme was in the works, calling for a Contra assault on Puerto Cabezas to establish a provisional government there, with contingency plans for U.S. air and naval bombardments to save the landing force from a disaster resembling the Bay of Pigs.[10]

Against this backdrop, we made our way toward Puerto Cabezas. It was already getting late on the third day as we approached the steepled church and rickety shacks of Yulu, where the peace process between the Miskitos and Sandinistas had begun. It seemed an opportune place to put in for the night. A patrol of Miskito fighters, distinctive in their bluish-green fatigue shirts and shoulder-length hair, ambled along the rutted thoroughfare alongside Sandinista soldiers. By now nearly half of the estimated 2,000 Miskito guerrillas who had taken up arms against the government had joined the peace process. They said everything was *tranquilo*, but I couldn't help but notice they seemed a bit on edge. They suggested we speak with the village preacher named Eagle, and they pointed down the lane to a cabin set on stilts high above the soggy ground.

Eagle Ignacio was a slim man, in his late forties, with a faint moustache and graying black hair. He wore a wide-brimmed felt hat and a pair of tear-drop sunglasses. I got a good feeling about him straight away. He spoke broken Spanish, but his soft-spoken manner exuded humbleness and honesty. He invited us to stay with him, his wife, and their two young sons, and he showed us up the stairway and into his house. Two sandy-haired dogs greeted us at the entrance with insistent nuzzles, tails wagging happily. Eagle's wife smiled from the far corner, where she was bent over a steaming pot on a woodstove. A sarape hung in a doorway at the rear, evidently leading to the family's bedroom. The furnishings were sparse: an uncovered plank floor, a few chairs, and a simple wooden table. On top of it sat a well-worn copy of *la Santa Biblia*.

The main population centers on the other side of Nicaragua were steeped in Roman Catholic tradition. But Moravian missionaries from Central Europe evangelized the Miskito villages along the rivers and lagoons of the Atlantic side, from the mid-nineteenth century onwards. In my travels throughout the Miskito Coast, I'd come to appreciate the importance of the Protestant faith for the Indigenous inhabitants. A white-washed, wooden-frame Moravian church marked the center of every community, and it served as the communal meeting place. As the local Moravian pastor, Eagle was among the most respected citizens of Yulu, with his finger on the pulse of village life.

After a dinner of chicken, rice, and beans, we sat in the glow of a kerosene lamp with Eagle and Kooha, a shaggy-headed Miskito fighter, who came by to check on this strange pair of American journalists who'd driven from Managua. Kooha said he was one of the first Indigenous commanders to accept the ceasefire, and he was now in charge of six rebel groups that were running joint patrols with Sandinista soldiers in the area. "A lot of people say we are a bunch of cowards for accepting the ceasefire," Kooha said. "But the very best Miskito fighters are here." Kooha recounted the raid he'd led on a sawmill in the neighboring hamlet of Sukatpin three years earlier to avenge a Sandinista attack. Despite the peace agreement, he remained skeptical of the central government's intentions. "When we get autonomy and the Sandinistas leave, that's when we'll believe they mean it."

Kooha bade us good night and disappeared into the darkness. Eagle's wife and his two boys had been lingering in the shadows. She motioned us back to the table for an evening snack of coffee and sweet bread. Delico, one of Eagle's sons, shyly approached, seeking the warmth of his father's embrace. *"¿Cuantos años tenés?"* I asked him. I realized from his searching eyes that he didn't understand. "He's nine," Eagle said. Delico did not know Spanish, Eagle explained. Only Miskito. That was the case for most people in Yulu, he said, which made them uneasy when Sandinista officials from Puerto would come to conduct business.

"My older sons—they speak Spanish." Eagle sighed. "Or they spoke it, anyway." He hadn't seen either of them in three

The road to Puerto Cabezas, Nicaragua, 1986.

Miskito rebel, Puerto Cabezas, Nicaragua, 1985.

Miskito preacher Eagle Ignacio, Yulu, Nicaragua, 1986.

years. "Remember what Kooha said about leading the sawmill workers to safety?" In truth, Eagle said, after burning the sawmill, Kooha's fighters kidnapped all 120 workers, including his sons, Lamsin and Tolontino, and herded them away to the camps in Honduras. "I haven't heard anything from them since. I just pray to God they're alive." A long pause ensued. "Kooha can say what he wants about the Sandinistas," said Eagle, breaking the silence. "And it's true, they were very bad. But now they're doing a lot for us."

Eagle said he'd been listening to reports on the radio about the American warships offshore. All able-bodied men in Puerto Cabezas had been called up to dig trenches in the bluffs overlooking the beach. He disappeared into a back room and emerged with a Vietnam-era M-14 rifle. The Sandinistas had given it to him. "In case the Americans invade," he said. Or in case Miskito fighters still allied with the Contras attacked Yulu.

The next day, Eagle led me out onto the plains beyond town to collect firewood. A thunderstorm moved across the horizon to the east. "It's raining in Waunta," he observed. I noticed another storm to the south and pointed toward it. "Ah, and it's raining in Layasiksa, too."

I asked Eagle to complete a circle, pointing in all directions around the horizon at what he knew to lie out there. As he did so, Eagle traced the boundaries of his universe. Over there was Haulover. Then Maniwatla, Karatá and Sukatpin. No east or west, north or south. I asked him where the United States was. His face went blank. "Right up there," I laughed and pointed straight into the sky overhead.

"Very good," he cackled, clutching his sides. "Very funny." Then I waved toward the north and said it was that way but many, many days' journey away. "Hum," he answered, "I thought it would be over there, where Puerto is." He nodded eastward.

It took me a second, but then I understood. An invasion or offshore bombardment would come from that direction. "You're right," I said. "It's over there, too."

Sandinista Popular Army troops, Amaka River Valley, Nicaragua, 1987.

# EIGHT

# Hunting Down the Sons of Reagan



**O**ur **Bulgarian C-rations** had run out. From time to time a soldier produced a stray can of greasy pork or chocolate he'd been saving up. It was impossible to keep such coveted goods a secret amid hundreds of voracious soldiers. It was immediately devoured, as if by locusts.

For days we'd been following the Amaka River north toward the border of Honduras, in pursuit of Contra rebels. Along much of its course, the river was shallow enough to trudge across, barely knee deep. When we reached a bend where it widened into a deep, gently swirling pool, Lieutenant Noel Talavera rummaged around in his backpack and withdrew a snorkeling mask. "We will not starve," he said with an ironic smirk and pulled the pin on a hand grenade. The muted explosion sent a plume of spray high into the air like a geyser. Talavera dove in and surfaced moments later, clutching a pair of twelve-inch bass. "You'd think they would float," he said. "But they don't." It was for such eventualities that Talavera brought along the mask. He tossed in another grenade and dove again, retrieving three more fish. He expended a few more grenades, collected more fish.

It wasn't nearly enough. Captain José Berríos, the battalion's affable commander, dispatched a squad to scour the forest. They returned an hour later with a tapir—a large, long-snouted animal with a gray hide so thick it took a dozen bullets to drop it. They had to hack the beast into quarters, lashing the hunks of flesh to poles they carried on their shoulders like pall bearers. I was relieved they hadn't returned with monkeys. The forest was alive with their hoots and chatters. To Berríos I recounted a story I'd heard from a friend about another unit that had run out of provisions in the forests of Nueva Guinea, far to the south. When soldiers assigned to hunting detail shot a monkey, its relatives descended from the trees in droves. Amid shrieks and waving fists, the monkeys hauled off their fallen comrade. The men just stood there dumbfounded. "I'd rather eat tapir," Berríos said deadpan.

We'd made it into the depths of the jungle aboard wave after wave of Soviet-made Mi-17 helicopters, ferrying three separate battalions of the Sandinista Popular Army (EPS) into the far reaches of northern Jinotega Department. By sheer chance, I had run into Talavera at the staging area back in San José de Bocay nearly two weeks before. I'd gotten permission to join the mission back in Managua, but I had no idea how big it would turn out to be. The scene was a whirlwind of cinematic proportions. Platoons of camouflaged soldiers lined up at the edge of an immense clearing. Helicopters circled, landed, and took off. Over the roar of the engines, Talavera shouted: "Come with us!" I had permission to join whatever unit I wanted, so I instantly agreed. He was still the Santos

Sandinista Army operation, Amaka River Valley, Nicaragua, 1987.

López Irregular Warfare Battalion's second-in-command, still as friendly and obliging as ever. It had been two years since I'd last seen him. By now the Santos López and several other Irregular Warfare Battalions, called BLIs, had been trained in airmobile tactics. The Sandinista Air Force had acquired a growing fleet of Soviet-supplied helicopters, making it possible for elite battalions to deploy quickly and to avoid the roadside ambushes that had been their Achilles heel when they moved in long convoys through the mountains.

It was April 1987, and the Contras were decamping their sanctuaries in Honduras for the interior of Nicaragua, flush with $100 million in aid approved by the U.S. Congress. The rebels were under pressure to take and hold territory inside Nicaragua, something they had been unable to do in nearly six years of war. Determined to thwart those efforts, the Sandinistas went on the counterattack, mobilizing the Santos López and two other BLIs to hunt them down and throw them back into Honduras.[1] But in the logic of escalating warfare, in which each move from one side was matched by a countermove from the other, the fresh aid package from the U.S. included some 200 shoulder-mounted Redeye missiles.[2] The heat-seeking projectiles were making the skies over Nicaragua decidedly more dangerous to navigate.

"We're heading into combat!" the pilot shouted over the *whoop, whoop, whoop* of the rotors as we prepared to depart the base at Bocay. "If we take fire and someone is hit, only the *compañero* next to him should help. No one gets out of his seat. A sudden shift in weight, and we'll all go down." I'd stifled any doubts about joining the mission up till that moment. Now it was too late. The helicopter slowly lifted off, struggling under the weight of the fifteen fully outfitted soldiers crammed into its belly. We barely cleared the trees at the end of the field. We maintained that altitude the rest of the way. We headed north over unbroken jungle, just above the treetops. It was how the Soviets and Cubans trained Sandinista pilots. The idea was to give enemy ground forces no advance warning of the aircraft's approach, minimizing their ability to set up and shoot. Still, I saw plenty of hilltops on our flanks that would have provided abundant opportunities for a shooter to bring us down.

That first night, I slung my hammock out on the battalion's leading edge, where advance scouts set up ambush positions beneath towering ceiba trees. I had just stretched out when the jungle erupted in gunfire. Red tracer rounds crisscrossed the darkness. I frantically tugged at the zipper on my jungle hammock. I tumbled to the ground, groped for my boots. I was terrified of being caught barefoot, unable to flee, if our position got overrun. Bursts of gunfire and obscenities flew back and forth. "Eat shit, mercenary motherfuckers!" the Sandinistas yelled. *"¡Piricuacos!"* the Contras taunted. "Filthy communist dogs!" A young recruit crawled to where I sat, struggling to get my boots on. "Come with me," he said and led me on hands and knees to shelter at the base of an enormous tree. Gradually, the bursts tapered off. In retreat, the Contras shouted: "¡*Somos los hijos de Reagan!* We are the sons of Reagan! It was interesting how they embraced such a moniker, even as they strived to project an image of themselves as a homegrown guerrilla force.

In contrast, Sandinista soldiers, at least those who believed in the revolution their weapons were defending, called themselves *los cachorros de Sandino*—"Sandino's cubs." Augusto César Sandino was the Sandinistas' progenitor, the guerrilla fighter who tied up U.S. Marines in a costly and prolonged war during the late 1920s. He inspired the founders of the Sandinista National Liberation Front (FSLN), and they went on to topple the Somoza dynasty in 1979. Despite the conventional trappings of the current-day EPS, their guerrilla past was much in evidence in the depths of the Amaka jungles. Talavera and battalion commander José Berríos were both from the mountains of Jinotega and were both veterans of the war against Somoza, as were all the company commanders I met during the two weeks I spent with them in the jungle.

Sandinista Army officer, Amaka River Valley, Nicaragua, 1987.

Contra fighters, Quilalí, Nicaragua, 1987.

One moonless night Berríos and Talavera showed me one of the many lessons they had learned as guerrilla fighters a decade earlier. "See these luminescent bugs?" Berríos asked. Until that moment, I hadn't paid much attention to the glowing green specks that zipped through the darkness around us. Berríos captured one in his cupped hands and delicately released it into a clear baggie. The bug was the size of a beetle, a good bit larger than a lightning bug. Berríos waved the baggie over his head. The glow of the imprisoned beetle attracted more of them. Soon Berríos had captured a dozen. "This is how we moved single file at night," he said. "You put one of them on your back, and the person behind could see it and follow." An entire squad could stick together, Berríos explained, undetected by the enemy. The bugs in that baggie were so bright I could scribble my notes by their glow.

Everyone was on edge. Soldiers cocked their rifles at the snap of a twig, shouting: *"Who goes there?"* We refrained from lighting campfires after dark. Only flashlights dimmed by red filters were permitted. Those measures didn't keep U.S. spy planes from finding our positions—and perhaps relaying them to the Contras. Many nights, the stillness was broken by the drone of aircraft passing overhead. "Archer!" Berríos yelled, alerting one of the SAM-7 specialists to ready an "arrow"—a heat-seeking missile. But the jungle canopy was too tight to allow a clear shot. The planes, said Berríos, were either CIA-operated flights to resupply the Contras or U.S. Air Force surveillance missions to pinpoint Sandinista troop movements. "They've probably been reporting our positions to the *guardia*," said Berríos, referring to the Contras. That might have explained why the battalion hadn't clashed with the rebels since that first night; they were using tactical intelligence to steer clear of us.

There was little the Sandinistas could do about it, because Nicaragua's military lacked the fixed-wing aircraft that could have kept its skies free from such intrusions. That was largely because the U.S. had threatened to bomb Nicaraguan airfields if the Sandinistas tried to bring MiG jets in from the Soviet Union. In the Fall of 1984, around the time of Reagan's reelection, hysteria in Washington over the possible arrival of fighter jets in Nicaragua reached fever pitch, with the President's lieutenants portraying them as offensive weapons that would destabilize the region.[3] The White House could not acknowledge the jets' defensive value to the Sandinistas; doing so would have required it to own up to sending clandestine flights over Nicaraguan territory in violation of U.S. and international law.

It was not only their insurgent past that informed the mindset of Sandinistas like Berríos and Talavera; they also saw themselves as the potential backbone of a future guerrilla army, should the *yanquis* invade. A U.S. strike may have seemed unlikely from the Stateside perspective, but the possibility seemed very real on the ground in Nicaragua. Low-flying American planes were crossing its airspace with impunity, the U.S. was conducting near-continuous military maneuvers in Honduras, and our warships plied the Atlantic and the Pacific just offshore.[4] Ever since the start of the Contra War, the Sandinistas maintained that the rebels' true purpose was to create the pretext for a U.S. attack. By 1985, the Defense Ministry had drawn up elaborate plans for such a contingency. Those plans called for elite battalions like the Santos López to morph rapidly into a rural insurgency that would bleed the gringo occupiers.[5]

Not all the recruits were committed revolutionaries. Many were not particularly political, and, when alone, some complained of abuse at the hands of overzealous non-commissioned officers (NCOs). One soldier named Amilcar said he was disgusted by rampant ass-kissing among his fellow conscripts who were angling to get time off, maybe even a free vacation to Cuba. My presence among them was a matter of intense curiosity. Who was this gringo in their midst, taking photographs, jotting notes? I was an exotic creature who shared their food, their hunger, the unremitting slog through

Sandinista Army sergeant with a monkey's head, Amaka River Valley, Nicaragua, 1987.

Sandinista Army soldiers, Jinotega Department, Nicaragua, 1987.

Marlon Ortega (center) with Sandinista media colleagues, Amaka River Valley, Nicaragua, 1987.

this inhospitable jungle. We joked together, laughed. My presence was a morale booster, like a house guest who breaks the monotony of a family's daily grind and keeps everyone on their best behavior. Among the more ideologically pure, however, I was an object of suspicion. "How do we know you're not CIA?" asked Guillermo, the battalion's dour political commissar, as we took a break in the steamy forest. "You don't," I said. "But I stand out too much. It's far more likely that you'd be a CIA agent than me. You'd have much better cover." After that he said nothing more about it.

I was the only American there, but I wasn't the only documentarian. A trio of Nicaraguan recruits were doing double duty as media-combatants. I met them one afternoon when they came into our camp. A shy young man named Marlon Ortega toted a video camera on one shoulder and an AK-47 on the other. He was with a sound tech named Gustavo and a still photographer named Oscar. The three were fulfilling their military service as media specialists for the Defense Ministry. Marlon told me he hoped to work at a TV station once he returned home to Managua. We exchanged phone numbers, promising to stay in touch.

Berríos received word via two-way radio that the main Contra force had retreated northwards; it made little sense for the battalion to continue on foot. Orders came to locate and clear a hilltop landing zone for helicopters to extract us. For two days the troops laid into the woods atop a knoll like a marauding hoard, felling trees with machetes and axes. As the forest thinned, a helicopter appeared overhead on the third day and lowered a chainsaw and can of fuel at the end of a rope.

The work proceeded quickly after that. But there was growing apprehension among the troops. What if all the racket tipped off the Contras, giving them time to move into position with their Redeye missiles? Marlon seemed spooked. He suggested another possibility: With the choppers flying so low to the ground, couldn't the enemy bring one down with just a burst of gunfire into the cockpit, killing the pilot and sending it into a tumble?

It was a cloudy morning when the helicopters swooped in to retrieve us. We stood at the edge of the clearing as the first came clattering in, maneuvering between the high trees on either side of the landing zone. The rotors sent woodchips flying like a spray of stinging bullets, forcing everyone to shield their eyes. Except for Talavera. The diving mask affixed to his face, he guided the choppers on to the hilltop, one at a time. I sprinted to board one of them and watched the barren knoll recede out the window with a mixture of relief and trepidation. At a bustling staging area in the middle of nowhere a half-hour later, I took leave of Talavera, Berríos, and the Santos López, hopping on a southbound helicopter.

Marlon Ortega's fears were not unfounded. Just days after we parted ways, the helicopter he and Gustavo were aboard was shot down, and they plunged to their deaths. It took me more than a year, but eventually I framed the photograph I'd made of him with Gustavo and Oscar in the jungle. I set out to find his mother, whom I tracked down in a working-class neighborhood near Managua's Eastern Market. She was still dressed in black when she came to the door. She invited me to sit at the kitchen table. She clutched the photograph to her breast and wept, again and again wiping her tears from the glass protecting Marlon's image. Besides a small headshot from grade school, she said, she had no other pictures of her son. "It's as though you have brought him back to me," she said. "He was such a good boy."

Dead Salvadoran Army soldier,  San Francisco Javier, El Salvador, 1989.

# NINE

# Shot Out of Nowhere



**I'd been in Central America nearly six years**, and the odds were beginning to catch up with me. No more than twenty feet away, my friend Cornel lay dying. The bullets were zinging hard and fast, pinging off the concrete and cobblestones. How weird, I thought, that my life would end this way. No photographic flashbacks. No cool, clear idea of what my mission was about or what I was doing there. Not a thought of how I would be remembered or what people would say. No. What I felt was a resounding self-condemnation, a unanimous jury crying *"Guilty!"* as I sprawled on the ground and considered how things would unfold in the coming minutes.

No decisive vision of self-preservation or self-sacrifice came to me. No heroics. I looked down at my blue jeans and bluish-green Banana Republic field shirt. With these clothes on, I thought, I'm a goner. As soon as the soldiers top the rise, they're going to take one look down their gun barrels and take me for a guerrilla, straight up. They will leave no witnesses. Because they'll also pop our driver, Julio, huddled in the dust nearby, and Kees, Cornel's producer, who is draped across Cornel's body, signaling with a thumbs-down from across a space of twenty lethal feet that Cornel is fading fast, maybe already dead.

Gentile and Arturo were out there somewhere. I'd last seen them when they dashed off in pursuit of a pair of guerrillas, disappearing beyond a tangle of brush at the edge of town. That was when all of us might have still gotten out alive. But now, we were pinned down, and Gentile and Arturo were God knows where.

Ten minutes before—or was it only a minute?—a shot rang out. At the same instant, Cornel let go an "UUGH!" He staggered, fixed me with a look of horrified surprise, and dropped to the ground. That first shot opened a ferocious fusillade that was still filling the air with a death knell, like a million snapping castanets.

It all fell apart so quickly. Just minutes ago, a cluster of friends had stood on the back corner of town high-fiving each other over the war footage, photographs, and experience we had just captured. It would make the international news clips. It would make for dramatic shots in the news magazines. It would make for great storytelling back in Managua, where all of us were friends, in the audience of colleagues who hadn't been there. It promised to be one of those tales we would tell and retell in the service of nurturing our mystique as fighters for truth battling the odds to expose the mendacious propaganda that sustained morally repugnant policies and those who crafted them.

By Spring 1989, the U.S. had expended hundreds of millions of dollars on the war effort in El Salvador. Throughout the decade, El Salvador had been the third-largest recipient of U.S. aid, after Israel and Egypt. By the time the war ended in 1992, an estimated 75,000 would be dead or disappeared.[1] A million people had been uprooted from their homes and fled the country, nearly half of them to the United States. The military and security forces were responsible for the vast preponderance of victims. As the war progressed, the army's ranks had doubled, then tripled and nearly quadrupled.[2] Still, nearly ten years into the war, the Salvadoran government and its U.S. backers were no closer to vanquishing the rebels of the Farabundo Martí National Liberation Front.

The FMLN had managed to survive, despite the mounting escalation and steady introduction of new weapons systems. Aerial surveillance had limited the guerrillas' ability to mass forces for large-scale attacks. An expanded fleet of helicopters also enabled the army to launch surprise attacks deep inside rebel-controlled redoubts.[3] Under moderate Christian Democratic President José Napoleón Duarte, elected to a five-year term in 1984, death-squad killings and other abuses had diminished. Modest economic and land reforms had blunted the appeal of rebel demands for revolutionary change. Still, either by forced recruitment or voluntary enlistment, the rebels continued to replenish their ranks. They continued to procure the weapons to arm those recruits. They could still count on the core of civilian supporters in their rearguard sanctuaries to provide food and logistics, despite intense bombardments and helicopter-borne incursions by ground troops. They also had carried a campaign of terror of their own in the backcountry, or perhaps it could have been called counterterror, executing a dozen mayors they suspected of attempting to reinvigorate paramilitary death squads in their communities.[4]

On that harrowing day in San Francisco Javier, Usulután, I was to get a close-up view of these developments. It was Election Day: March 19, 1989. Duarte's five-year term was coming to an end. Despite its modest accomplishments, his administration had been unable to end the war. It had been tarred by the rightwing opposition as corrupt and soft on communism. The far-right Nationalist Republican Alliance (ARENA), founded at the start of the decade by renowned death-squad leader Roberto d'Aubuisson, had long argued against paying lip service to niceties like human rights. The time was long overdue to take the gloves off, its militants believed. Still, ARENA had an image problem. To cleanse it, the party tapped a softspoken businessman, Alfredo Cristiani, to run at the top of the ticket, and he was poised to win.[5]

As Election Day drew near, legions of journalists once again converged on El Salvador. I arrived from Guatemala, where I'd moved in late 1988. Several old friends came in from Nicaragua, including Bill Gentile and *Time* photographer Arturo Robles. We all found our way to the Camino Real Hotel, still the press corps' nerve center and principal rendezvous spot in El Salvador. Also visiting from Managua were friends from the Dutch television network IKON: Cornel Lagrouw, Kees Elenbaas, and Annelies Helwegen. Of the three from Holland, I knew Cornel the best. He was tall and good-looking, his sandy hair styled in a James Dean pompadour I envied. The corners of his mouth were invariably curled in a beguiling smile, and he was always game for adventure. At a party two nights before the elections, we shared drinks and laughs and agreed to meet back at the hotel to watch the election results and celebrate.

Without sharing our plans with the Dutch or any other journalists, Bill, Arturo, and I decided we'd head to eastern El Salvador, where the grim realities of the ongoing war might offer a counternarrative to the stage-managed cliché of voters braving bullets to cast their ballots in favor of democracy. That was the U.S. Embassy's official line, never mind that this was a stunted democracy where serial killers roamed free and only half the spectrum of political views was represented on the ballot.

Bill had rented a small Suzuki Jeep and hired Julio to drive it. Together, the four of us made for Usulután, where years of repression and counterinsurgency had done little to quell the restiveness. We checked into a cheap hotel just

FMLN rebels, San Francisco Javier, El Salvador, 1989.

Salvadoran Army troops on the frontlines, San Salvador, El Salvador, 1989.

off the square in the departmental capital and spent a sleepless night, punctuated by the thud of mortar rounds and the prattling of machine guns as the rebels launched an attack on the city's two military garrisons. The lights flickered, then went out altogether. The city was plunged into darkness. We gathered briefly in the courtyard to share a cigarette. But there was nothing to do but return to bed; it would have been suicidal to venture out into the pitch-black streets.

We checked with the innkeeper on our way out the door the next morning. "Trouble? You're looking for trouble?" he asked incredulously. "Well, I'd say head for one of those towns up there above the coast road, like San Agustín or San Francisco Javier." I was thinking the same thing. San Agustín was where I'd met the guerrillas that day with Richard Wagner and the CBS crew in October 1983. Like dozens of other towns that girded El Salvador's midsection, you never knew what you'd find in either village. Even after nine years of fighting, neither the army nor the FMLN had the wherewithal to maintain a permanent presence there. The remaining civilians inhabited a kind of twilight-zone existence, caught between the two sides. It was the kind of place where bullets, not ballots, were likely to define the cadence of the day's events.

We first heard the guns while still on the Coastal Highway. We turned onto the dirt road that led toward San Francisco Javier. It was the height of the dry season, and soon we were gagging on fine, lunar-like dust that seeped through the rolled-up windows and floorboards. The hammering of guns got louder. Above the ridgeline up ahead a spotter plane circled lazily like a vulture.

We stopped to ask a campesino what was going on. "Combat," he said. "It's been going on since dawn. I wouldn't go up there if I were you." That was all we needed to hear. Julio floored it. Onward we went.

Combat had subsided by the time we reached the outskirts of town fifteen minutes later. We passed a cluster of gun-toting teens smoking cigarettes and sipping Cokes on a shady doorstep. Remarkably, no one stopped us as we bounced up the cobblestone street. There were no sentries, no one wondering what we were doing there. I was startled by their youth: None looked older than sixteen, far younger than most of the rebels I'd met a few years earlier. It stood to reason; the longer the war dragged on, the deeper into the population each side needed to go for recruits. The other thing that struck me was their weaponry: Nearly all of them were porting AK-47s from the Eastern Bloc. This was a new development.

Throughout the first seven or eight years of the war, the only rifles seen in the hands of FMLN fighters were U.S.-made M-16s, the occasional Belgian FAL, and West German G-3s, which had been standard issue for El Salvador's National Guard. In its White Paper of 1981, the U.S. Department of State alleged that the Soviet Union had engineered the transfer of thousands of M-16s captured or left behind during the Vietnam War to the FMLN via Cuba and Nicaragua. The allegations were key to winning Congressional approval to arm and train the Nicaraguan Contras, who were supposed to interdict weapons shipments to El Salvador.[6] For its part the FMLN said its fighters were capturing most of their weapons from the Salvadoran Army, and there was ample evidence to support that claim. Entire inventories of U.S.-supplied armaments had been lost in rebel ambushes and attacks on barracks and armories.

But as we proceeded further up the main street of San Francisco Javier I saw more and more AK-47s, with their distinctive banana shaped magazines, in the hands of the teenaged rebels. They couldn't claim to be taking these from the army. Clearly, a major change had taken place.

As with most guerrilla conflicts the world over, the Salvadoran rebels fought with the same weapons used by the government they were trying to overthrow. At least until now. On a practical level, brandishing the same guns as the government insured a ready supply of ammunition, obtainable by force or bribery. Politically, there was the question of deniability: It made it more difficult for the government to prove the weapons had come in from outside.

Parallel processes in El Salvador and Nicaragua reflected this axiom. The Salvadoran guerrillas shouldered American-made rifles against a U.S.-supported regime; in Nicaragua, the CIA funneled Eastern-Bloc weapons to the Contras in their fight against the Soviet-supplied Sandinistas. But now, word had it that Salvadoran rebel agents were buying up caches of Eastern-bloc materiel from profiteering Contras in Honduras.[7]

Even if the Sandinistas were smuggling arms to El Salvador, corruption in the Contra ranks now provided a credible cover: The Salvadoran rebels could freely furnish recruits with fresh, Soviet-made arms without fear of backlash from the U.S. The irony was rich: The Contras, rather than interdicting weapons flowing from Nicaragua to El Salvador, had become a conduit. And if that wasn't the case, it was curious to note that the new administration under President George H. W. Bush made scarcely a peep when ever-greater quantities of AK-47s turned up in El Salvador.

Villagers were just emerging from their homes as we reached the center of town. On a side street, a dead soldier lay sprawled face-up. An enormous sow had also been killed, and several young men strained under its weight as they loaded it onto a wooden cart. But no one touched the soldier. Some barefoot kids led us to the schoolhouse, where they showed us trashed urns and smoldering ballots with which the citizens were to have exercised their franchise that day.

I pulled out my microphone and approached the rebels. They said the balloting was part of the regime's counterinsurgency campaign, and they had chosen to exercise a kind of veto power. "The elections aren't going to solve any problems," said one as he puffed on a cigarette. His face and olive t-shirt were spattered with dried blood. Hadn't he heard that the FMLN's high command had issued an order to fighters to desist from attacks to allow people to vote? He shrugged. Among the guerrillas was a scrawny kid. A deep furrow creased his forehead. He was barely taller than his M-16. I asked how old he was. Twelve, he said. How long ago did he join the guerrillas? Four years ago. What led him to join? The

army had come to his house and shot his mother and father, he said, right before his eyes.

Just then another car with "TV" taped to its windshield bounced up the street. The Dutch journalists piled out. Pure coincidence. We hadn't told them of our plans, but they had a similar inclination to head to the war zone. They'd heard on the radio about fighting in San Francisco Javier and had come to have a look. Bill led Cornel around the corner to the dead soldier. Cornel rolled, panning up from the body to include gawking villagers and a passing guerrilla in the shot. The soldier—name unknown, life story untold—had become a prop in the theater of war.

Bursts of gunfire erupted down the hill. In the distance, a dozen figures were running toward us up the street. "Who are those guys?" Gentile shouted. It was hard to tell at first. They were silhouetted against the harsh light. But as they drew closer, we saw that they were the same guerrillas we'd passed on our way into town an hour earlier. The army was counter-attacking, and they were in retreat. As the rebels reached us, Cornel pushed Annelies into an open doorway. "Stay here till we come back!" he yelled over the gunfire.

We followed the rebels up the hill to the back corner of town. One of them took casual aim at the spotter plane, which had suddenly returned, and squeezed off a burst. The plane veered off into the distance and a lull set in. We milled about on the knoll, reloading cameras. An eerie stillness settled over the village. "Guys, our time here is rapidly drying up," Gentile said. "Those motherfuckers are just over the ridge." But just then, Arturo took off after a pair of rebels who raced toward the army attackers, and Gentile followed.

Back in my earlier days in 1983 and 1984, I'd learned from more experienced journalists that it was safest to venture into El Salvador's conflict zones with a small and select group of friends, maybe just one or two others. Once a group got larger than that, it had the potential to get out of hand: too difficult to coordinate, too easy to lose track of where everyone was, too

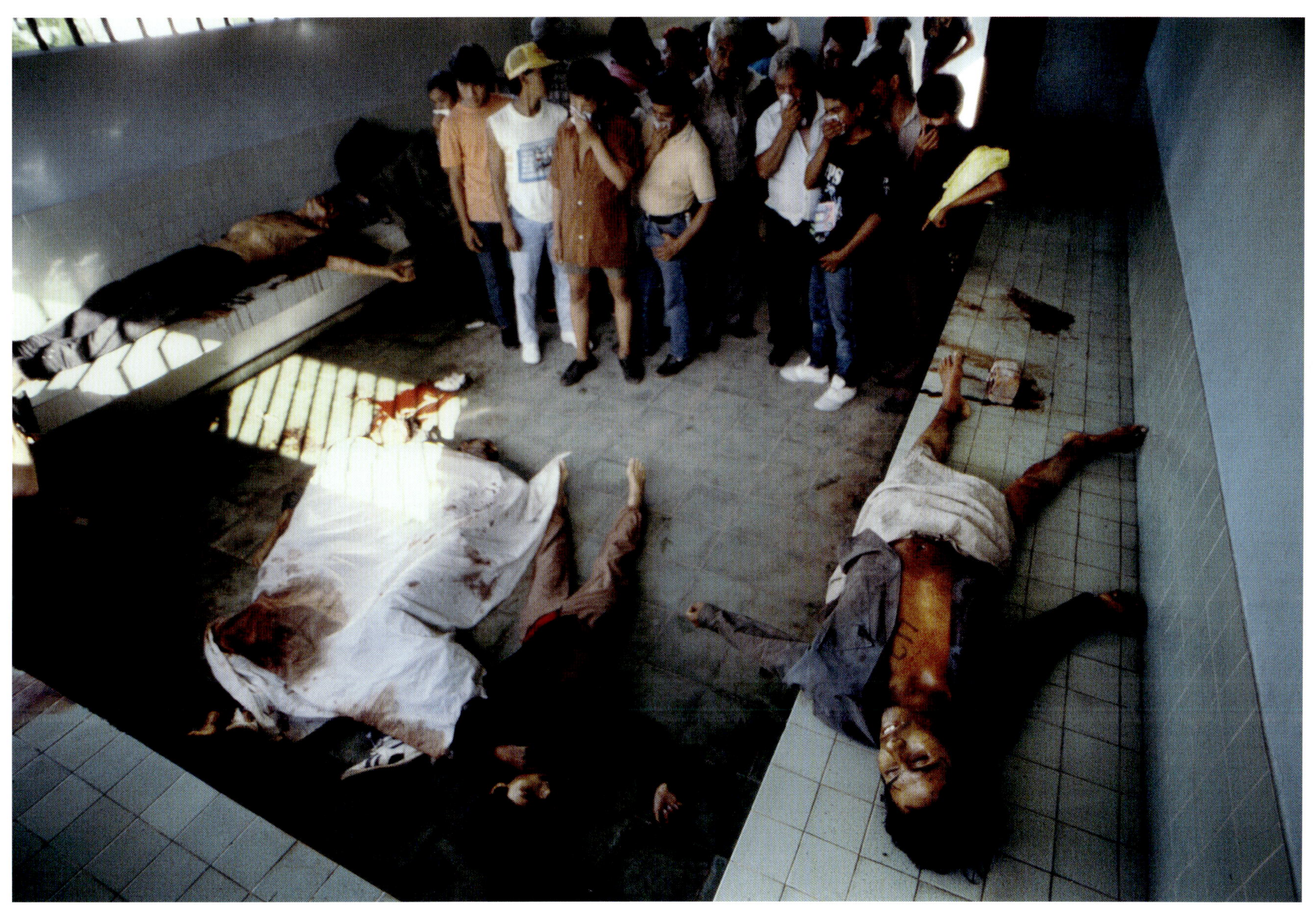

Metropolitan morgue, San Salvador, El Salvador, 1989.

FMLN guerrillas on high alert, Mejicanos District, San Salvador, El Salvador, 1989.

great a chance that something could go wrong. The appearance of the Dutch crew in San Francisco Javier had scrambled the odds. With their arrival, the size of the group had doubled, and the risk climbed exponentially.

I stood there with Cornel and Kees, staring into the screen of foliage beyond which our friends had vanished. It was as though we were mesmerized by that impenetrable view. But then, something told me to move. As if by instinct, I broke off my gaze and took a few steps back toward Julio, who had taken cover behind a ledge. If I'd been thinking clearly, I would have told Cornel and Kees to do the same. But I wasn't, and I didn't.

That's when I heard the crack, like a large branch being shorn from a tree. In the same instant Cornel let out a gasp. His eyes locked on mine in a wild plea. He spun on his heels and fell. Kees and I were frozen in place. There was nothing we could do. Gentile and Arturo finally returned, dodging bullets at full tilt. Bill took charge, barking orders for our retreat. We carried Cornel down the hill, each grabbing an arm or a leg. Annelies emerged from the doorway, wailing in disbelief at the sight of Cornel's inert body. Arturo and I piled into the Samurai with Julio. The others followed in the Dutch crew's car.

Groundfire erupted from the trees along with the simultaneous whoosh of bullets. Julio floored it. Minutes later, we came under fire again, this time from an army helicopter that was closing fast behind us. I leaned out the window. Over my shoulder, I saw the muzzle flash of its guns and braced for the bullets. They kicked up dust in a spurt alongside us. The road out followed an open ravine, with one side sheltered by an embankment and the other side wide open. It was along the open side that the chopper now approached.

Julio slammed on the brakes, and we dove out the doors. The helicopter hovered so close I could make out the visor of the door gunner's face. We were at his mercy. I furiously waved a white cloth and braced for the burst that would ignite the jeep's gas tank and blow us away. Then, suddenly, the helicopter jerked away and disappeared.

We jumped back into the jeep and raced on. We couldn't help but kick up clouds of dust along the parched trail, making us easy pickings if the chopper returned. Within five minutes, we heard the terrifying beat of the rotor blades. The chopper was once again upon us, just as a peasant's hut came into view around the bend. Julio plowed the jeep into the farmyard. We dashed into the house. The owners—a farmer and his wife—implored us to leave. The beating wings were now directly overhead. *¡Por favor, salgan de aquí!*" they shrieked. "Please get out of here!" We ignored them. Once again the terrifying chop faded away, and we resumed the journey.

At the hospital in Usulután City, orderlies laid Cornel on a stretcher and rushed him indoors. But he was already gone. The attending doctor showed us where the bullet had passed through his right bicep, then entered his abdomen, through a purplish hole the size of a dime. It had lodged near his heart. There was almost no blood. It was hard to believe a life so large could vanish so quickly through a hole so small. I kept replaying that moment in my mind. How that gunshot had kicked off that unending fusillade. It bore the mark of a sniper. He'd likely been lining me up in his crosshairs as well. And then I stepped away.

Two Salvadoran journalists, Reuters photographer Roberto Navas and a television reporter named Mauricio Pineda, were also killed by government forces while covering the elections. Another Reuters photographer, Luís Galdámez, was severely wounded. We heard that a U.S. Embassy spokesman later poo-pooed the helicopter attack, telling reporters the gunner could have blown us away if he'd wanted to. That may have been true, but it was a laughable assertion, coming from someone who rarely if ever would have ventured beyond the Embassy bunker in anything less than an armor-plated vehicle. Like most U.S. officials in El Salvador, the spokesman wasn't just viewing the world through the distorting lens of the Cold War; he was looking at it through two inches of bullet-proof glass.

Contras hanging raw meat, La Piñuela, Nicaragua, 1990.

# TEN

# End of the Road



**"W**ho are these guys?" came the anxious voice of photographer Jeff Perkell from the back seat. It was hard to say, but a snap judgement was in order. Six armed men stood in our headlights, blocking the road. Were they Contras? Sandinistas? Or a hybrid of both, a new breed of post-war, professional highwaymen?

We were four people in an SUV on a dirt track of a road in the middle of nowhere. Night had already fallen. Throughout years of war, it never would have occurred to us to travel on a backcountry lane after dark in the heart of Nicaragua's Central Highlands. But the ceasefire between the Contras and Sandinista government had lulled us into a false sense of security. Now, a half-dozen men were pointing AK-47s straight into our windshield, waving us to a halt.

"Don't betray any fear," Gentile said, dousing the headlights and snapping on the jeep's interior lights—standard procedure when approaching a roadblock of armed men at night. "These guys are going to fuck with our minds. Scott, if anything, make like we're pissed off. They're keeping us from completing our journalistic mission."

"Keep your hands where they can see them," I told Perkell, a relative newcomer with little experience in the countryside, without taking my eyes off the assailants. I quickly sized them up: Their faces were shrouded in red-and-black bandanas, the signature colors of the Sandinistas. But I'd been around a lot of Sandinista troops, and I couldn't picture them holding up travelers at gunpoint. It just wasn't their M.O. But maybe, after they slipped the authority of commanders, they were capable of anything. For the most part the Sandinistas I had come to know took their role as soldiers in a popular army to heart. The bandanas seemed like a ruse. "They must be Contras," I admonished. "Remember, do not under any circumstances call these guys *compas.*"

To address someone as a *compa*, short for *compañero*, was how the Sandinistas called each other. To use the word tagged you as an *internacionalista*, a communist sympathizer. An hour before, when we were among a group of Contras gathered in a U.N.-supervised ceasefire zone, Perkell had mistakenly blurted it out. It had been a harmless faux pas then, among rebels in the process of disarming. He even made the Contra commander laugh. But it could have proved fatal; the Contras had killed a dozen foreign volunteers working for the revolution, including the idealistic American engineer, Benjamin Linder. Here, there was no telling what would happen in the coming minutes. One thing was certain: There was no margin for any kind of error. "Jeff, let me and Scott do the talking," Gentile said.

Seven years before, I had arrived in El Salvador with $50 in my pocket, two small bags, and CBS credentials. I had no idea how long I would stay or how I would manage. Two years later, in 1985, I moved to Nicaragua, as public attention shifted toward the escalating confrontation between Washington and the Sandinistas. At times it had seemed almost inevitable that the U.S. would invade, given President Reagan's visceral loathing of the Sandinistas, the nonstop American military exercises encircling Nicaragua, and his unwavering commitment to the Contras, who proved incapable of seizing power on their own. But, in the end, Washington managed to dislodge the Sandinistas at the ballot box. With the Contras poised to be turned loose to renew the war, President Daniel Ortega lost his reelection bid to the U.S.-supported opposition candidate, Violeta Chamorro. Her inauguration was to be held the next day in Managua.

The war had exacted a staggering toll in blood and treasure. More than 40,000 were dead.[1] Proportionally, that would have amounted in the United States to two-and-half million. Economic losses were incalculable. Gone was the idealism of the revolution's earlier years. The grand social experiment was finished. Nicaragua had been brought to its knees. The Sandinista Revolution was over.

The Contras had been gathering in U.N.-designated safe havens to disarm. As soon as Chamorro was sworn in, they'd turn in their weapons and go home. One such enclave was located in the department of Chontales, in the Central Highlands about a four-hour drive from Managua. We resolved to have a look. For Bill Gentile and me, this was to be a final jaunt together, a kind of commemorative. Both of us were heading home to the States. This would be our last hurrah. We were joined at the last minute by Perkell, who happened by Gentile's house just as we were getting ready to leave and decided to come along.

Like the country itself, the journalists like us who had held on through the decade to witness the end of the Reagan Administration and the Contra War were beset by uncertainty.

Where to now? For what purpose? And perhaps most unsettling of all: How to find an encore to this? How would we ever come close to replicating the intensity and camaraderie we'd experienced in covering this story? Would we ever again find a place and a people we cared about so much about, that we knew so well, that had embraced us so warmly?

It was already mid-afternoon when we reached the hamlet of La Piñuela, a collection of clapboard shacks assembled around a broad clearing. Several men in U.S.-issue camouflage huddled beneath a barren tree, roasting a steer they'd evidently requisitioned from a local farmer. They used cleaning rods from their AKs as barbeque skewers. Ribbons of raw meat hung from the tree limbs to cure, imparting a disquieting air to the scene. We asked the Contras about the coming peace and what they planned to do when they returned to the dells and valleys from which they hailed. They seemed pleased the war was over but confused about their prospects, just like us.

Dusk was gathering by the time we wrapped up. Under normal circumstances we'd have stayed put for the night. But we assumed the ceasefire would afford us some measure of protection. Besides, we hadn't provisioned ourselves for an overnight trip. We bid farewell and pulled away.

Now, an hour later, the silhouettes drew close upon us in the darkness. "Get out of the car!" one of them snarled, pointing his rifle between my eyes. The war may have been over, but in a split-second, it dawned on us that we were faced with something new: combat-hardened men with rifles and no chain of command to answer to.

"What's the problem?" I asked emphatically to the guy as he yanked open the door and pulled me from the jeep. "We're journalists. American journalists."

"Yeah, but you guys support the Sandinistas," the gunman sneered.

"We have nothing to do with the Sandinistas," I countered, as though he couldn't have hit upon a more searing

Contra fighter, Quilalí, Nicaragua, 1987.

insult. "On the contrary, we've just come from interviewing *los comandos*!" I lavished emphasis on *los comandos*. The Contras liked to be called commandos. It conferred a certain mystique. They liked to think of themselves as soldiers in the service of a higher cause—God, the liberation of Nicaragua, the preservation of Western civilization. *Comando* had the perfect ring to it.

The Contras and their American backers devoted a good deal of attention to propagating the commando myth, for the consumption of the Contras' own fighters and the Nicaraguan peasantry. Broadcasts on the Radio Liberación—a 50,000-watt clandestine station beamed nightly into Nicaragua from El Salvador—opened and closed with "*Comandos de la Libertad*," a rousing battle anthem replete with recorded machine-gun fire and grenade explosions.[2] It was intended to impart a sense of gallantry and purpose.

"Comandos?" The gunman's voice brightened. "Do you carry orders from them?" Sadly, we did not. But seeing an opening, I pressed ahead. "Look, we've just come from La Piñuela. There are many commandos there. Their *comandantes* have made important declarations, and we're in a rush to report them to the world! Democracy has triumphed!" He said nothing at first, just spun me around to face the jeep. Shit, I thought, I'd gone too far. Could he smell the BS through his bandana? Maybe I'd gotten it wrong. Maybe these guys weren't Contras after all.

"Get your hands up," he said. I felt his paw slide into my hip pocket and pry my wallet loose. I checked an impulse to resist. "Decent money," he croaked. I had collected a debt from Gentile that morning and had carelessly brought the money along. Now it was gone. Another set of hands jerked the Casio watch from my wrist. "*Por la causa,*" the voice said. "For the cause," I agreed.

Out of the corner of my eye, I saw that Gentile and Perkell were getting similar treatment. At the back of jeep I could see the silhouette of yet another gunman. "You, in the military boots, come with me," barked the silhouette. His rifle was pointed at the fourth member of our party—an AP photographer named John we'd only just met in La Piñuela. He had come in from Mexico for the inauguration and had decided to venture out to make images of the Contras.

He'd never been in Nicaragua before, had never been in a war zone. For some reason, he had turned down a ride with whomever had brought him there, and he needed a lift back to Managua. I baulked. He was wearing military-style jungle boots and black commando pants, stuff straight off the shelves of an Army-Navy store. You learned early on to avoid wearing such gear in the countryside. Maybe if you were embedded with one side or another but otherwise no. It raised too many questions about who you were and what you were up to. Against our better judgment we agreed to take him with us.

"You, with the boots," the voice repeated to the photographer. "Come with me." The shadowy figure started to march John down the road into the blackness. In a flash, I could see everything unravel. Once he got John alone he would shove him to his knees, then put a bullet in his head. I could not allow that to happen not only for his sake, but for all of ours. After they killed him, a feeding frenzy would ensue. They would finish us off.

I stepped between the shadow and his quarry. "Look," I said, "the señor is wearing this stuff because he bought it in the States. Up there, they sell it to anyone. He's strictly a journalist, and he has done very good work for democracy in Nicaragua." The presumed Contra backed off.

Another of the assailants had boarded the jeep and was rummaging around the back seat. "I really like this bag," he said. He was holding up my reporting bag. Curiously, he didn't seem interested in my cameras or recording gear. I emptied the bag and presented him with it. "It's of excellent quality," I said. "Made in England." He tried it on his shoulder. "We will put it to good use," he assured me. I stepped

Contra fighters and an evangelical preacher,
Yamales, Honduras, 1989.

backwards off the running board, back into the shadows beyond the glow of the jeep's interior lights. It was time to make our move.

"Well, brothers," Gentile spoke up. "We've given you what we can offer. We need to get going. What about it?"

Silence ensued. Finally, one of them said: "Okay, you can proceed. Keep your inside lights on. Don't look back. Keep driving." We climbed aboard and pulled away into the night. The vehicle rocked us back and forth along the rutted road.

We continued in silence, processing what had just happened, how close we'd just come to the end. But we would make it back to Managua. We would make it back to our friends, our girlfriends, our wives. We would see the sun come up tomorrow. I would be in Miami by Friday, bringing nearly seven years in Central America to an end.

And as our headlights fell upon the bend in the road up ahead, where we'd vanish forever from the sights of the guns still trained at our backs, I couldn't wait to get there.

Sandinista Army troops, Estelí Department, Nicaragua, 1990.

Detained looter, Baghdad, Iraq, 2003.

# ELEVEN

# In Search of Enemies



**T**he border crossing was surprisingly desolate at 9:00 a.m. Beyond an empty parking lot was a wasteland of shifting sand. The hustlers and hawkers who attend such transit points the world over were absent. A Kuwaiti official in a barren concrete outpost stamped my passport. There was no one to do the same on the Iraqi side. There was no passport control whatsoever. I waited as the sunlight turned blinding white. I was thinking my ride would never come when a gleaming new GMC Suburban pulled up. A burly man in his mid-thirties climbed out. He had short brown hair, and a pair of wraparound shades concealed his eyes. He said his name was Ra'ad. He offered a thick paw, opened the tailgate, and motioned for me to toss in my stuff. I decided to keep my newly purchased Kevlar helmet up front with me, thinking it might come in handy.

It was early July 2003, four months after the U.S.-led invasion of Iraq, and we would follow the same route Coalition forces had taken in March in their race to Baghdad. Ra'ad's English was sketchy, mostly monosyllabic, but I understood that he had been making the run on a regular basis. "How's the road?" I asked. I didn't mean the condition of the pavement. "Half and half," he said, tilting the open palm of his free hand back and forth. "Many Ali Baba." He was referring to a broad assortment of criminal elements that were rapidly proliferating in post-invasion Iraq. I'd heard the highway was rife with bandits and carjackers since the U.S.-led coalition had ousted Saddam Hussein. But the other land route to Baghdad, from Jordan, was rumored to be worse.

I cast a wary eye out into the desert. Dust devils swirled across the flatlands like the faint ghosts of tornadoes. Mirages danced on the horizon. Transmission towers dotted the landscape, punctuated by orange splashes where oil wells were flaring off methane gas. We passed men in a repair truck hoisting a power cable that had fallen on the roadway. "Sabotage," Ra'ad explained in a single word.

Traffic was sparse. A flatbed escorted by a camouflaged Humvee went past, hauling a backhoe. There was the occasional seventies-model Ford, an ancient, exhaust-belching Chevy. It seemed that our brand-new SUV might make an attractive target for "Ali Baba." I discreetly scratched my calf, where I'd taped an envelope stuffed with $1,700 in cash. Another $1,000 in hundred-dollar notes was tucked into a money belt around my waist.

"What do we do if we're stopped?" I asked. "No stop," Ra'ad said. He opened the console between us and gestured to a Smith & Wesson .38. He cranked the volume on a tape of hard-pounding Arabic pop, fished into his shirt pocket and offered me a Marlboro. He'd been a security guard in the Iraqi Army during the First Gulf War, he told me.

Reveling in the plaudits that attended the route of Saddam's forces from Kuwait in 1991, President George H. W. Bush declared then that America had "kicked the Vietnam syndrome" that had sapped the nation's confidence and prestige.[1] Even so, the elder Bush promised to avoid another prolonged, unpopular, and unwinnable guerrilla war against an amorphous enemy. That was why he had stopped short of going to Baghdad to drive Saddam from power.

But that lesson was clearly lost on his son, George W. Bush, now in the White House, and the neo-cons he'd arrayed around him—men and women convinced of the rightness of their cause, even as they lied and dissembled and led the United States into what many observers and scholars believe to be the biggest foreign-policy blunder in the nation's history.[2] Among the cast of characters were die-hard Cold Warriors who got their start during the 1960s in Vietnam, Cambodia, and Laos. Others plied their trade in the Central America theater of war, subterfuge, and deception that I covered from 1983 to 1990. A handful—John Negroponte, James Steele, Colin Powell, and, yes, Henry Kissinger—spanned all three engagements. In the autumn of their careers, they arrived in time to participate in one way or another in Operation Iraqi Freedom, code name for the invasion and subsequent occupation of Mesopotamia, and to indulge once again their shared faith in American supremacy.[3]

We reached Baghdad as the sun dissolved into a deep crimson band spreading across the western horizon. Ra'ad dropped me at the Palestine Hotel after navigating a maze of concrete barriers that forced us into a series of S turns, overseen by a U.S. Army tank whose turret gun pointed directly at us. I paid Ra'ad and bade farewell. He started back through the same gauntlet and disappeared behind a high blast wall that offered a hint of the chaos that was beginning to engulf the country.

It had been a tumultuous time for me since leaving Central America. I'd gotten married, moved back to my hometown in upstate New York, and fathered three sons. I hustled to find a way forward as a freelancer with a family to take care of. I traveled to Russia to witness the collapse of the Soviet Union and later returned to report on the rise of organized crime in post-Soviet Russia. I went to work for the local Gannett newspaper, covering the police beat and influx of new immigrants from Bosnia, Burma, and Belarus who were revitalizing my crumbling Rust Belt city. I journeyed to the Arctic and the Amazon to report on the assault of the resource-hungry global economy, seemingly turbocharged by communism's demise, on the world's last great wilderness regions and their frontline Indigenous defenders.

No matter the story—whether the aftermath of a massacre in Chalatenango or the struggle of Cree caribou hunters in Quebec's Far North to block a massive hydroelectric project—I'd come to realize that at heart I am a field reporter, that nothing gives me a greater sense of purpose than to venture into places of difficult access to pursue dramatic stories of critical interest that would otherwise remain untold, their protagonists unseen and unheard. When the chance arose to join author Peter Bergen as his photographer on assignment in Afghanistan for *Vanity Fair*, I seized it and then managed to cobble together two other gigs that would take me through Pakistan and Kuwait to Baghdad.

I found my way to the Al Safeer, a small hotel on the east bank of the Tigris, just across the river from the "Green Zone," the heavily fortified compound that occupied four square miles in the heart of the city. Within its walls, Saddam had built lavish palaces, parade grounds, and government buildings. It now served as the nerve center for the Coalition Provisional Authority, as the U.S. christened the occupation government it led.

*New Yorker* writer Jon Lee Anderson, whom I'd first met twenty years before in El Salvador, had booked me a room next door to his, with our adjoining balconies looking down on the river. Jon Lee had reported extensively from Iraq in

A defaced mosaic of Saddam Hussein, Baghdad, Iraq, July 2003.

recent years, and he was among a small group of Western journalists who remained in Baghdad during U.S. Secretary of Defense Donald Rumsfeld's "shock and awe" smart-bomb campaign that preceded the ground invasion.

"It's a creepy atmosphere," said Jon Lee, briefing me on the local state of affairs. "You hear about people getting killed, violent car jackings, serious criminality." The Americans were sandbagging themselves in, hunkering down in the Green Zone, he said. "Bush has exposed his Achilles heel. This is a perfect place for Al Qaeda to pop Americans." As if to goad the nascent insurgency, a jocular George W. Bush that same day hinted that he was itching for a fight, telling reporters at a White House ceremony to *"bring 'em on"* when asked about the growing number of attacks on U.S. forces.

Within a few days, I arranged through the Army's press office to join a foot patrol through central Baghdad. It was early July, and the pavement already sizzled at 10:00 a.m. as I set off with a squad of GIs down the street, trailed by a herd of kids tugging at our sleeves. "Hey, meester, how are you?" they playfully shouted. "Hey, meester, what you name?"

We turned off the street and entered Saddam's Ministry of Information building. It had been repeatedly bombed during the early days of the war. Its walls and windows had been blown out, but its skeletal structure remained intact. The inside was thoroughly trashed. There was no carpeting to be seen, no furniture to speak of. All that remained were busted filing cabinets, papers strewn everywhere, and smashed plate glass that crunched underfoot. As we picked our way through the darkness, ducking twisted shards of metal that dangled from the ceiling, it felt as though we'd entered a surreal, dystopic world conjured in Ridley Scott's imagination.

We heard Arabic voices in excited whispers echoing through a stairwell. Corporal Blake Gibson wheeled around with his M-4 and turned on the flashlight mounted on his rifle. Three young men, their hands and faces blackened with soot, were descending the stairs dragging burlap bags. "Get down!" Gibson barked. Their sacks were stuffed with copper wiring. "Are there other Ali Babas?" Gibson asked, pointing up the stairs. "How many Ali Babas—two, three, four?" The looters were "zip-stripped"—bound with plastic zip cuffs—before we dashed up the stairwell. Several flights up, we came upon another pair of young vandals as they laid into a phone box with a hacksaw.

In all, eight looters were marched back for processing at the Assassin's Gate, a sandbagged checkpoint at the entrance to the Green Zone. Too bad the troops didn't engage in this kind of crackdown from the very beginning. Back in April, Rumsfeld had arrogantly sloughed off the looting. "Freedom's untidy," he said.[4] Now, Iraq's infrastructure lay in shambles, the Iraqi people were seething with resentment, and a guerrilla resistance had begun to congeal.

The U.S. forces, trained in the kind of blitzkrieg maneuvers that had brought them swiftly to Baghdad, had little idea of how to restore order or keep the peace. As in Vietnam, they soon had the sense of being out of place, strangers in a very strange land.[5] Though Iraqis hadn't exactly welcomed the American military as liberators, many were relieved to be rid of Saddam, cautiously optimistic that life would soon get better. But officials in Washington seemed oblivious to the gathering storm, as resentment and resistance to the occupation began to percolate. The attacks mounted, the soldiers' paranoia grew, and the Iraqis' initial goodwill was squandered.

The patrol vanished into the Green Zone with the detainees. While I waited for my driver to collect me at the Assassin's Gate, I began exchanging small talk with the unit's 1st Sergeant, a tall man wearing sunglasses, body armor, and close-cropped hair. His name was Alec Lazore, and he was second-in-command of Alpha Company, 2nd Battalion, 6th Infantry Regiment of the 1st Armored Division. He told me about the dash north from Kuwait four months earlier, that his men were getting antsy, having been away from their base in Germany for eight months. Just as my ride pulled up, I asked him where he was from. "A small town in upstate New York you've never heard of." Try me, I said. "Utica," he answered. I laughed. My hometown. I could even picture the block where his family lived. That cemented a bond. He told me to come back whenever I wanted. I did the next day and for many more days after that. It turned out to be an education.

On the first operation I went with the company on a nighttime raid to an apartment complex that housed government workers and former Ba'athist Party members. What ensued showed me just how quickly excessive zeal can turn potential friends into bitter enemies. Residents at the "Red Apartments," as the Americans called the compound, had been standoffish when the troops had walked through the development on daylight patrols. Kids had teased them: *Hey, meester, where you from?* And they'd been shot at with a BB gun from the upper stories, Blake Gibson said. He relayed this tale with a gravitas that surprised me, as though the BBs posed mortal danger. It was time to look behind closed doors in the Red Apartments, he assured me. Surely, they were hiding something. As Alpha Company went through a rehearsal for the raid outside the Italian-marble palace that now served as their billet, one soldier muttered, "All we're going to do is piss off a lot of people." It was an accurate prediction.

U.S. Army guard post, downtown Baghdad, Iraq, 2003.

U.S. and Afghan troops, Nangarhar Province, Afghanistan, 2003.

Shortly after dark, we disembarked from a fleet of armored personnel carriers, sprinted across a dimly lit plaza, me fast on the heels of the point man, rolling video, and entered the ten-story complex. Soldiers pounded on doors and pushed their way in. I judiciously allowed three or four men to go head of me before I entered. "Get down! Get the fuck down!" they shouted as occupants dropped to the floor. They zip-stripped every male under the age of fifty. They rifled through drawers, overturned mattresses, smashed open armoires when residents didn't promptly unlock them. Where occupants were away, troops took sledgehammers and crowbars to their doors, busted them open and tossed their apartments. All they managed to find was a single AK-47 and an ammunition clip, which were, in fact, legal for Iraqi families to possess.

Despite his protestations of innocence, Munjad Abdul Haqi, a middle-aged chemistry professor and a former officer in the Iraqi Army, was among the detainees led away by the soldiers. Three days later I went with an interpreter to visit his apartment. A woman dressed in abaya and hijab ushered me in, surprised that one of the Americans who raided their home had come back. Her husband still had not. "I'm worried sick," said Amira Abdul Amir, the professor's wife. "I haven't eaten for three days." His mother, dressed in a black chador, sat in the corner, tears streaming down her face. "He's a kind man," she sobbed. "We're afraid, because we hear that people who are captured don't come back. They insult us more than Saddam did."

Alpha Company's commander, Captain Scott Nauman, told me that his men had turned Haqi over to Army counterintelligence to investigate possible links to a chemical-weapons program. Allegations of Saddam's supposed quest to develop weapons of mass destruction (WMD) had served as one of George W. Bush's and U.K. Prime Minister Tony Blair's principal justifications for going to war. No evidence ever turned up to prove the existence of WMD. But the supposition that they

had to be *somewhere* had sent the U.S. military at every level on a fool's errand to seek them out. Alpha Company of the Second Battalion, 1st Armored Division, was no exception.

There was no need for subterfuge when America went to war in Afghanistan in 2001 following the 9/11 attacks. The U.S. enjoyed broad support among the world community for its mission to hunt down Osama bin Laden and root out his Al Qaeda jihadis from their mountain strongholds along the border with Pakistan. And there was observable delight among the Afghan people to be rid of the Taliban. But U.S. officials found themselves in continual contortions as they invented and reinvented the rationale for invading Iraq. Besides the WMD argument, they were also fond of trying to pin at least part of the blame for 9/11 on Iraq, going to great lengths to concoct a nonexistent link between Saddam and bin Laden. Among the standard-bearers of this factual sleight of hand was Bernard Kerik, tapped by the Bush Administration to head the country's Interior Ministry and "stand up" the new Iraqi Police. As New York City's Police Commissioner two years earlier, Kerik had personally witnessed the horror at Ground Zero, and he saw the invasion of Iraq as a kind of settling of scores. Among the assignments I had pulled together before leaving the States, *AARP The Magazine* commissioned me to do a profile of Kerik in text and photographs, and he was generous in the access he provided and the doors he opened during my time in Baghdad.

"The attack was committed by some very bad people, supported by people in other countries," Kerik told a graduation ceremony one morning at Baghdad's Police Academy, invoking the other main rationalization for invading Iraq. "One of the people that supported them was the regime of Saddam. The people that attacked the Towers threatened our freedom in the United States, just as Saddam took your freedom away."[6]

In any case, Kerik said, Saddam's crimes—the mass disappearances, the persecution of Shi'a and Kurds, and the

U.S. Army sergeant, Mansour district, Baghdad, Iraq, 2003.

summary executions—were on an order of magnitude that wholly justified the U.S.-led invasion. "When I think about weapons of mass destruction, there was only one weapon of mass destruction in this country, and it was Saddam and his regime," he says. "And it gives me a lot of pleasure to ride around this city and to realize that he's no longer here, and he's not coming back." It didn't matter that no WMD were ever found, that Saddam had nothing whatsoever to do with the 9/11 attacks, that the United States had flattened a country on false pretenses or, as more generous critics put it, on faulty intelligence.

There was a through line to the dissembling, the deceit, and the disinformation, going back nearly a half-century to Vietnam. An overblown incident in the Gulf of Tonkin in 1964 provided legal cover for President Lyndon Johnson's sharp escalation of the war in Vietnam. Twenty years later, President Ronald Reagan's State Department served up similarly flimsy evidence in its White Paper to launch the Contra War in Nicaragua and persuade a squeamish Congress to support a murderous regime in El Salvador. And now, another two decades on, officials were engaged yet again in deliberate obfuscation over the authorship of the 9/11 attacks, as well as a nonexistent WMD program, to justify the invasion of Iraq. It can be said that the widespread distrust of government and the proliferation of conspiracy theories and the "Deep State" claptrap that we witness today owe at least some of their force to the failure of our highest officials to level with the American people, dating back to the Vietnam War and Watergate.

A blast from a distant bomb shook the windows one morning as we sat on cots in the former Republican Guard palace where Alpha Company was billeted. "This is urban guerrilla war," Lazore said with a touch of foreboding as the windows rattled again. But despite the counterinsurgency campaigns the U.S. had waged in Vietnam and Central America, this was a war that Lazore and most of the occupying force in Baghdad were ill-prepared to fight. Recent years had seen the U.S. rack up a string of quick victories won with overwhelming force: in Panama, Kosovo, and the First Gulf War. Exactly how to wage a guerrilla war, or a counterinsurgency, may have been forgotten, but the mendacity, arrogance, and deception that attended the entire operation from the top down were all too familiar.

If there was one man in Baghdad who hadn't forgotten how to fight guerrillas though, it was former U.S. Army Colonel James Steele. A highly decorated veteran of Vietnam, Steele during the mid-1980s was head of the MILGROUP, as the Pentagon's detachment of fifty-five Green Beret advisors in El Salvador was called. I'd gotten to know Steele back then, a lanky man with sandy hair and a slight Texas twang. I'd sat in on many of his briefings at the U.S. Embassy, had interviewed him several times, and had seen him in the field in the aftermath of guerrilla attacks on government forces. He remembered me right away when Kerik introduced us at his offices in the Green Zone, but luckily, he seemed to have forgotten the sometimes-contentious nature of our interactions from those days in El Salvador.

Only during the Iran-Contra hearing in late 1986 would we find out that, during his tenure in El Salvador, Steele was facilitating Oliver North's secret and illegal arms pipeline to the Nicaraguan Contras out of Ilopango Air Force Base, just east of the capital. He retired from the service after he was passed over for promotion for dissembling to Congress about his role in the Iran-Contra Affair.[7] Before he retired, he was put in charge of organizing a new Panamanian police force in the aftermath of the December 1989 invasion. Code-named "Just Cause," the invasion was later described as a "template" and "training ground" by Secretary of State Colin Powell and Vice President Dick Cheney for the later operations in Iraq.[8] Shortly after the invasion of Iraq in March 2003, Steele's old friend, Paul Wolfowitz, then-Deputy Secretary of Defense, offered him a job as advisor to the new Iraqi Police. In that capacity, Steele

Homesick troops, Fallujah, Iraq, 2003.

was tasked with creating an elite "special enforcement team" that would pursue "bad guys" of every description—kidnappers, carjackers, extortionists. Topping the list of targets were Saddam loyalists, called *fedayeen*, who were in the process of organizing an armed resistance to the occupation.

Steele invited me to come along on a mission. A few nights later, I found myself in the backseat of an SUV as we careened at breakneck speed through the dark streets of Baghdad, Steele in the driver's seat. Sitting alongside me was a man whose entire head was wrapped in a red-checked *kufiya* to conceal his identity. Steele called him the "source," and he had agreed to point out a man he said had fired an RPG at a Coalition convoy some weeks before.

The anonymous informant called to mind the CIA's notorious Phoenix assassination program in Vietnam. There, hooded informants were made to point out the homes of supposed Viet Cong cadre who were subsequently "neutralized." By 1971, CIA director William Colby disclosed in testimony to Congress that the Phoenix program had resulted in the elimination of more than 20,000 suspects.[9] It turned out that many of the victims had been misidentified, targeted for reasons of personal vendetta in some cases, in others because the informant was a VC double-agent working through his own blacklist of American collaborators.[10]

We were stopped at several Army checkpoints. "Hi boys," Steele told them, flashing his ID. "We're police advisors. We're on a mission in the area with the Iraqi Police." Each time they poked their heads through the window, their eyes alighting on the man sitting next to me with his head wrapped in the kufiya. Each time the soldiers waved us through.

We stopped in front of a low-lying building. A dog barked. Gravel crunched underfoot as we approached the target house, weapons drawn. All told there were about a dozen men in on the raid, including an FBI agent from New York and Steele's partner, an Iraqi-American police sergeant named Nouman Shubbar on leave from the Philadelphia PD. We

were in a rundown suburb of dirt thoroughfares and single-story houses, far from downtown Baghdad. The neighborhood was pitch dark, not a single streetlamp in service. It was two o'clock in the morning.

"Coalition forces! Open up!" Steele shouted and banged on the door. A bolt snapped back, and the door creaked open. We pushed our way inside. Women and children lay sprawled under blankets on the floor. We proceeded down a narrow hallway in darkness. Rats squealed. The passageway led to a loft occupied by several men. There was a heavy scent of body odor. Rousted from sleep, they descended a ladder in the glare of Steele's flashlight, hands in the air. The "source" fingered the suspect. He was led outside to the cars and an uncertain fate. Policemen were shouting and pointing their rifles in the direction of the rooftops. They were clearly anxious to get out of there.

We pulled out in a hurry. As we rounded a corner, gunfire erupted. Steele slammed on the brakes. We bailed out, dove for cover. Red tracers zipped past us, followed by a heart-thumping lull. We scrambled back into the vehicles and peeled out. The mission ended in a hospital hallway, where two Iraqi policemen were laid out on stretchers. Steele followed nurses into the ER, where they were treating a third casualty who'd been hit in the thigh.

Who had shot at us was a mystery. It was unclear if they had been insurgents or if we'd taken friendly fire from U.S. troops. As we waited in the brightly lit hospital corridor, the FBI agent paced back and forth, fuming over the lack of coordination between the various military units patrolling the zone. "You've got to be damned careful out there," he said. Referring to the American troops, he added: "They're ready to light up anything."

I was too young to have been in Vietnam. But I knew about the disposition of troops to shoot first and ask questions later. The My Lai massacre was the most publicized atrocity, but it was far from the only one.[11] By its very nature, guerrilla war presents special challenges. As Mao Zedong said and the Guatemalan colonels repeated to me, the guerrilla swims in a sea of ordinary citizens. Frustrated soldiers often fail to distinguish combatants from innocent civilians. In El Salvador, American-trained police forces and intelligence-gathering services morphed into death squads. Elite counterinsurgency battalions trained by U.S. Green Berets racked up several massacres in hamlets suspected of harboring sympathy for the FMLN rebels. U.S. officials had been complicit in their cover up.[12] As Iraq veered toward chaos, I feared the process would repeat itself again.

The Iraq campaign was only a few months old, but already, the patience of U.S. troops was wearing thin. Many soldiers just wanted to go home. When I visited the restive city of Fallujah, soldiers expressed outright contempt for the Iraqis. They were told they'd be welcomed as liberators; why were the locals so ungrateful? It didn't help that, like Vietnam, they found themselves in a bewildering land whose language and culture they did not understand and had no interest in trying to.

Russian troops invading Ukraine in 2022 were likewise assured by Vladimir Putin that they'd be greeted by the locals with open arms on his "special military operation." The conduct of U.S. forces in Iraq hardly resembled the ongoing brutality and indiscriminate attacks of the Russian occupiers in Ukraine. But the blatant illegality of America's unilateral move to invade Iraq has served Russian propagandists well, diluting U.S. moral authority in the global propaganda war taking shape between the forces of democracy and authoritarianism.

I was grateful when I made the list for a military flight out of Baghdad. I had no desire to brave the overland route to either Jordan or Kuwait. I'd been in Iraq for a month, but it felt a lot longer. Our C-130 ascended almost vertically in a tight corkscrew pattern to minimize the chance of getting hit with a shoulder-fired missile. Above the high-pitched whistle of air rushing over the wings, I could make out a conversation going on next to me between a British soldier who'd been stationed in Mosul and a private from the 101st Airborne. "It's all right," the American said to the Brit, summing up his deployment. "The only thing that sucks here is the weather—and dealing with Iraqis."

It could have been a scene from our doomed engagement in Vietnam, a GI on his way home, hoping he'd never lay eyes on an another "gook" for the rest of his life. What was the ultimate cost in lost and ruined lives there—not only of our own servicemen and women, but also among the people we set out to "save"? Then there were the countries of Central America—El Salvador, Nicaragua, and Guatemala—where the Cold Warriors in Washington waged proxy war, promoted mass murder, and covered it up.[13] Now they refused to acknowledge their own outsized role in the ongoing crisis at the Southern Border. It's as though their policies had nothing to do with the waves of immigrants fleeing those ravaged lands, year after year after year. It's as though none of it ever happened.

As our aircraft gained altitude over Baghdad, I thought back over the previous four weeks—everything I'd seen and everyone I'd met. There was one moment in particular that stood out, that I could not shake.

I was finishing up my visit with the family of the chemistry professor who'd been taken away by the soldiers of Alpha Company three nights earlier. His wife, Amira, stopped me at the door. "All my life I've had a single desire—to make the pilgrimage to Mecca," she said, looking me in the eye as my interpreter translated. "I don't care about that anymore. The thing I want now more than anything else is that, one day, you people in the United States will be made to suffer like we have suffered here."

Even now her words still haunt me.

U.S. Army patrol at twilight, Baghdad, Iraq, 2003.

**Press credentials** are the key for any journalist working at home or abroad. For a freelance journalist, it's critical to get a news organization to issue a press card or an official letter stating that she or he is on assignment for that particular news outlet.

Before I left the U.S. for El Salvador, I received authorization to report for CBS News Radio. I was issued a CBS press card and gear. I was also granted permission to use the CBS News bureau in El Salvador and to join the news team there.

With credentials from a news organization, the journalist then needs to get credentialed by local authorities. In Nicaragua, these documents were issued by the Foreign Ministry. In El Salvador, the ID came from the military. When I first got there, the credential was a letter-sized piece of paper, on which they'd staple your photo (page 156). We laminated the letters to preserve them from wear and moisture. The Armed Forces High Command later began to issue official press cards.

In El Salvador, it was also important to get an ID from the Salvadoran Foreign Press Corps Association (SPCA.) The SPCA card was useful to present when stopped by the guerrillas. Flashing the Armed Forces card would arouse suspicions, especially since the early versions of it looked identical to the ID provided to U.S. advisors, with the bearer's photograph taken against a red background.

The exception was Guatemala, where authorities were so suspicious of journalists that they refused to issue credentials of any kind. There, I had the good fortune to happen upon an international police convention, where organizers mistook me for a police officer and issued me an official ID. When stopped at military roadblocks, soldiers examined the ID and assumed I was an advisor. They would salute and send me on my way.

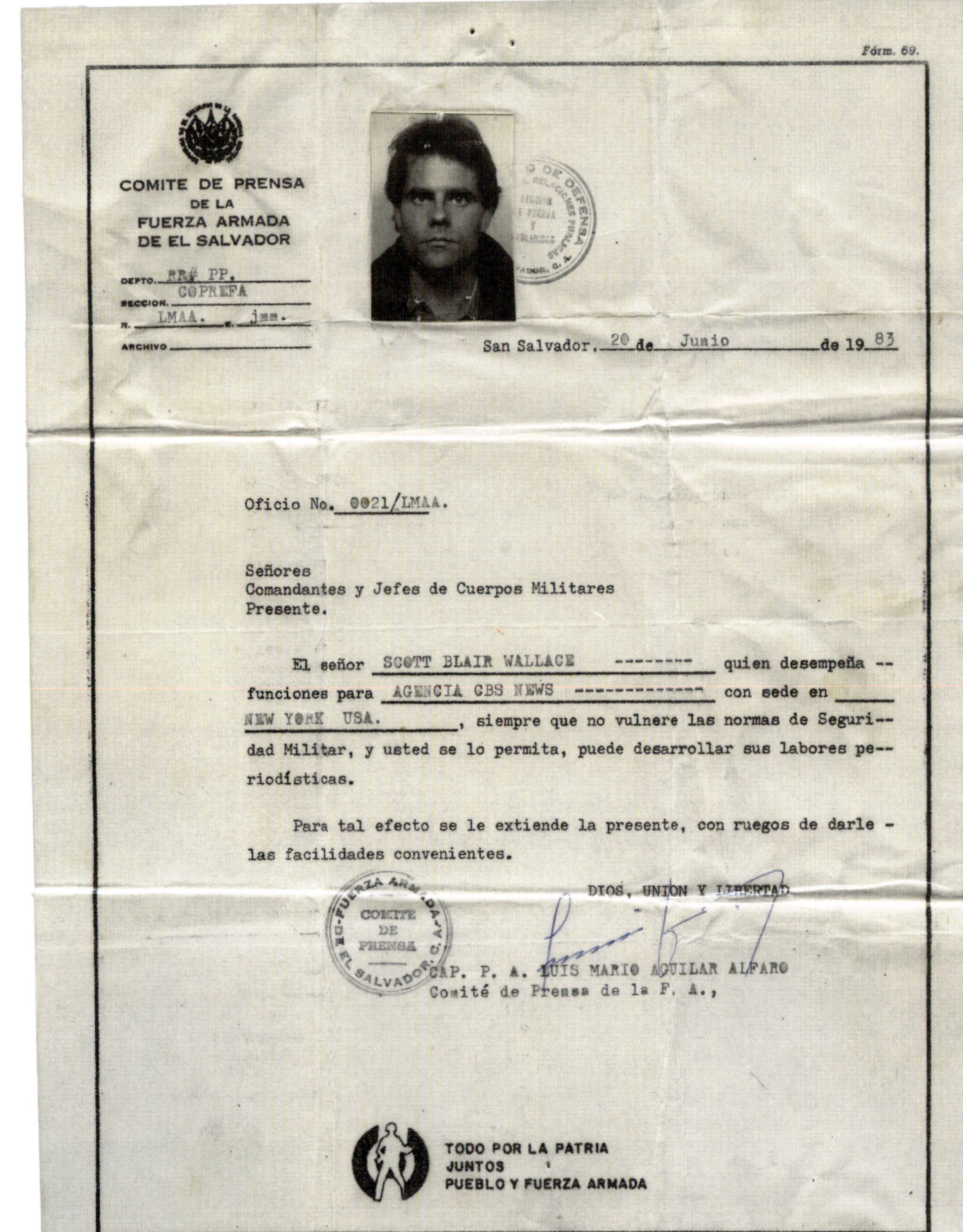

*Fórm. 69.*

COMITE DE PRENSA
DE LA
FUERZA ARMADA
DE EL SALVADOR

DEPTO. RR. PP.
COPREFA
SECCION. LMAA. jmm.
N.
ARCHIVO

San Salvador, 20 de Junio de 19 83

Oficio No. 0021/LMAA.

Señores
Comandantes y Jefes de Cuerpos Militares
Presente.

El señor SCOTT BLAIR WALLACE ——————— quien desempeña —— funciones para AGENCIA CBS NEWS ———————— con sede en _______ NEW YORK USA. ________, siempre que no vulnere las normas de Seguridad Militar, y usted se lo permita, puede desarrollar sus labores periodísticas.

Para tal efecto se le extiende la presente, con ruegos de darle — las facilidades convenientes.

DIOS, UNION Y LIBERTAD

CAP. P. A. LUIS MARIO AGUILAR ALFARO
Comité de Prensa de la F. A.,

TODO POR LA PATRIA
JUNTOS
PUEBLO Y FUERZA ARMADA

DEC 06 09.16

20058 CBS SAL

20058 CBS SAL

ST
C     CALLING SCOTT WALLACE
STANDBY FOR ATLANTA CONSTITUTION FILE

ZZZ

SAN FRANCISCO LEMPA, EL SALVADOR-  THE YOUNG BOY HAD BEEN LOOKING FOR
HIS FATHER SINCE THE EARLY MORNING HOURS. SHORTLY AFTER DAWN LAST
WEDNESDAY, HE CAME UPON THE DISFIGURED BODY LYING FACE DOWN BY THE
SIDE OF THE ROAD. SANTIAGO VITELIO ALAS, A 46-YEAR-OLD FISHERMAN
FROM THIS POOR LAKESIDE TOWN IN NORTHERN EL SALVADOR, HAD BEEN TOR-
TURED AND SHOT FOUR TIMES

YOUNG SANTIAGO, WHO HAD BEEN NAMED AFTER HIS FATHER, RAN BACK TO TOWN
TO TELL HIS SISTER AND NEIGHBORS. HIS MOTHER, ROAS CORRECTION ROSA
MIRIAM DE ALAS, HAD ALREADY LEFT FOR THE CAPITAL, HOPING THE FOREIGN
JOURNALISTS AT THE CAMINO REAL HOTEL COULD HELP. MAYBE THEY COULD USE
THEIR POWER TO GET HIM BACK. SHE FELT NO RESENTMENT; BUT AFTERALL,
IT WAS BECAUSE OF THE PERIODISTAS (ITALICS) -- THE JOURNALISTS --
THAT HER HUSBAND WAS IN TROUBLE. MAYBE THEY COULD USE THEIR POWER TO
GET HIM BACK. SHE PRAYED AS SHE PILOTED THE FAMILY'S SMALL BOAT
ACROSS LAKE SUCHITLAN THAT THE FOUR GUNSHOTS SHE HEARD IN THE NIGHT
DID NOT MEAN HER HUSBAND WAS DEAD.

THE MEN HAD COME TO THE HOUSE ABOUT MIDNIGHT.FIVE OR SIX OF THEM,
BRISTLING WITH RIFLES AND MACHETES, THIER FACES MASKED WITH RED
BANDANAS. AS ROSA MIRIAM DE ALAS LAY TREMBLING IN BED, THEY DRAGGED
SANTIAGO ALAS FROM HER SIDE. THE MEN TOLD ALAS THEY WERE TAKING HIM
FOR HIS COLLABORATION WITH THE PRESS. ABOUT 15 MINUTES AFTER THE MEN
LEFT WITH HER HUSBAND, SENORA DE ALAS HERAD THE SHOTS.

SENORA DE ALAS WOULD LATER RECALLL HER HUSBAND'S FEAR AFTER THE TRIP
DOWN THE LAKE WITH THE JOURNALISTS. TWO WEEKS EARLIER ON NOV. 15,
A GROUP OF SIX REPORTERS AND AN ABC TELEVISION CREW PRESSED ALAS FOR
HIS SERVICES. THEY WERE TRYING TO REACH THE SITE OF AN ALLEGED ARMY
MASSACRE NEAR THE WAR-RAVAGED TOWN OF COPAPAYO. THE ROAD TO COPAPAYO
WAS SAID TO BE MINED, SO THE REPORTERS DECIDED TO GO BY BOAT FROM
FROM THE TOWN OF SUCHITOTO ON THE SOUTH SIDE OF THE LAKE.

BESIDES FISHING ON LAKE SUCHITLAN, SANTIAGO ALAS MADE HIS A LIVING FO
R HIS WIFE AND SEVEN CHILDREN BY FERRYING PASSENGERS BACK AND FORTH
BETWEEN SAN FRANCISCO LEMPA AND SUCHITOTO. THE JOURNALISTS WERE THERE
BY THE SHORE WHEN HE LANDED WITH A GROUP OF PASSENGERS. HE HESITATED
AT THEIR OFFER. THIRTY COLONES (ITALICS), ABOUT $7.50, WAS A LOT OF
MONEY FOR ALAS. BUT HE NEVER VENTURED EAST TOWARD THAT END OF THE
LEAKE LAKE. THE PEOPLE SAID IT WAS DANGEROUS. AND IF THE AUTHORITIES
WERE TO FIND OUT THEY WERE GOING TO INVESTIGATE AN ARMY MASSACRE...
SOMETHING BAD COULD HAPPEN.

SALVADORANS HAVE LONG SINCE LEARNED THAT SURVIVAL DEPENDS ON AVOIDING
THE SUSPICION OF AUTHORITIES AND STAYING AWAY FROM DEAD BODIES,
WHOEVER THEY MIGHT BE. THERE MUST BE A REASON, AFTERALL, FOR THEIR
BEING DEAD. IT'S BEST NOT TO GET INVOLVED-.

SANTIAGO ALAS ACCEPTED THE RISK, AGREEING TO TAKE THE GROUP TO
COPAPAYO. THE TRIP DOWN THE LAKE WAS UNEVENTFUL. ALAS COULD HAVE

**I evolved a particular approach** to newsgathering during the years I covered the tumult in Central America. I went into the field with camera and tape recorder, notebook and pen. With the latter, I came to value taking meticulous field notes. I grew into a practice of writing as fast as I could while also assuring my scribblings were legible. I conducted most of the interviews in Spanish and translated them simultaneously into English as I wrote. In time, I came to realize that I was creating a retrievable archive—one I could call upon weeks, months, even years later, when I might need to write something besides the immediate news story. Indeed, I could neither have written the text portions of this book nor provided an accurate reconstruction of the events without these field notes.

When reporting for CBS News Radio, I always rolled tape for my interviews, whether with heads of state or landless peasants. I needed to capture the voices and ambient sounds that give radio its immediacy and evocative power. Once back in my office or room, I would pound out my scripts on a portable Olivetti typewriter, using carbon paper packs that created four copies. Each was a different color. The packs were indispensable in a broadcast newsroom, each sheet serving a different function: the white copy for the presenter's desk, the pink for the teleprompter, the gray for the producer, and so on. As a field reporter, I had no pressing need for all four copies, but I saved them in a folder, which I recently unearthed. During my first two years in Central America, I filed stories to the Atlanta newspapers via telex from the CBS bureau in San Salvador.

Things are very different now, but, even then, the business of newsgathering and filing stories was undergoing rapid change. During the mid-1980s, portable computers began to supplant the typewriter and telex for composing and sending news stories to headquarters. I bought my first computer in 1985, and I used it to file stories to U.S.-based media. (I continued to dictate stories by phone to notetakers for the U.K. newspapers—*The Independent* and, later, *The Guardian*—through the end of the decade.) Those early computers were slow, with barely enough memory to store a few pages of text, and we then had to connect our computers via a dial-up phoneline. It would take several more years for the Internet to hit full stride. We take for granted the speed and amount of information that now travels through the global information system that it is hard to remember how we managed to communicate before smartphones and computers.

Still, the fundamentals of reporting remain unchanged. There is no substitute for getting out in the field to observe and experience events with one's own eyes and ears. Eyewitness coverage by trained, ethical journalists remains the best antidote to the avalanche of disinformation, conspiracy theories, "alternate facts," and propaganda that threaten the public's ability to sift fact from fiction. I think it's fair to say, as Senator Dodd notes in the foreword to this book, that the survival of democracy and democratic values will depend in large part on the survival of a free and robust press.

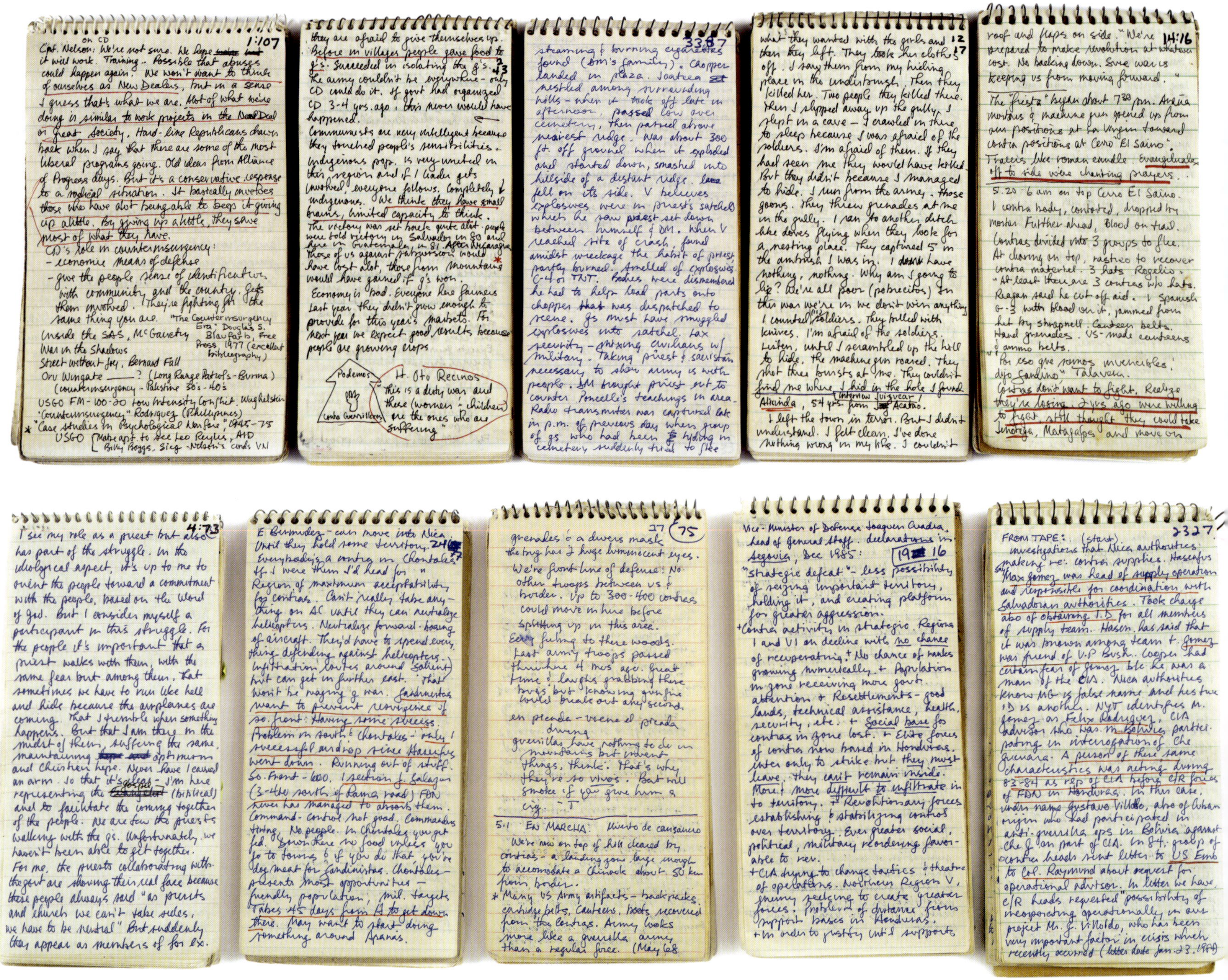

**[Notebook 1 — "1:107"]**

on CD

Cpt. Nelson: We're not sure. We hope ~~~~ it will work. Training — Possible that abuses could happen again. We won't want to think of ourselves as New Dealers, but in a sense I guess that's what we are. Alot of what we're doing is similar to work projects in the New Deal or Great Society. Hard-line Republicans drawn back when I say that there are some of the most liberal programs going. Old ideas from Alliance of Progress days. But it's a conservative response to a radical situation. It basically involves those who have alot being able to beep it giving up a little. By giving up a little, they save most of what they have.

CD's role in counterinsurgency:
- economic means of defense
- give the people sense of identification with community and the country. Gets them involved. They're fighting for the same thing you are. "The Counterinsurgency Era" Douglas S. Blaufarb, Free Press, 1977 (excellent bibliography)

Inside the SAS, McGarrety
War in the Shadows
Street without Joy, Bernard Fall
Orv Wingate ____ ? (Long Range Patrols - Burma)
(counterinsurgency - Palestine 30's - 40's
USGO FM-100-20 Low Intensity Conflict. Waghelstein
"Counterinsurgency" Rodriguez (Philippines)
* "Case studies in Psychological Warfare" 1945-75
USGO [Make apt. to see Leo Reyes, AID
[Billy Boggs, Sieg Nelson's cmds VN

**[Notebook 2 — "43"]**

they are afraid to give themselves up. Before in villages people gave food to g's. Succeeded in isolating the g's. 43 The army couldn't be everywhere - only CD could do it. If gov't had organized CD 3-4 yrs. ago, this never would have happened.

Communists are very intelligent because they touched people's sensibilities. Indigenous pop. is very united in this region and if 1 leader gets involved, everyone follows. Completely & indigenous. We think they have small brains, limited capacity to think.

The victory was set back quite alot. people were told victory in Salvador in 80 and here in Guatemala in 81. After Nicaragua those of us against subversion would have lost alot, those from mountains would have gained if g's won.

Economy is bad. Everyone here farmers. Last year they didn't grow enough to provide for this year's markets. For next year we expect good results because people are growing crops

[diagram: Podemos / contra Guerrilleros]  H. Oto Recinos "this is a dirty war and these (women & children) are the ones who are suffering"

**[Notebook 3 — "33 87"]**

streaming & burning cigarettes found (DM's family). Chopper landed in plaza. Soatrea nestled among surrounding hills - when it took off late in afternoon, passed low over cemetery, then passed above nearest ridge. Was about 300 ft off ground when it exploded and started down, smashed into hillside of a distant ridge. lava fell on its side. V believes explosives were in priest's satchel which he saw priest set down between himself & DM. When V reached site of crash, found amidst wreckage the habit of priest partly burned. Smelled of explosives. C-4 or TNT. Bodies were dismembered he had to help head parts onto chopper that was dispatched to scene. g's must have smuggled explosives into satchel. Lax security - mixing civilians w/ military. Taking priest & sacristan necessary to show army is with people. DM brought priest out to counter Poncelle's teachings in area. Radio transmitter was captured late in p.m. of previous day when group of g's who had been & hiding in cemetery suddenly tried to flee

**[Notebook 4 — "12 ... 57"]**

what they wanted with the girls and then they left. They took his clothes off. I saw them from my hiding place in the undbrush. Then they killed her. Two people they killed there. then I slipped away up the gully. I slept in a cave — I crawled in there to sleep because I was afraid of the soldiers. I'm afraid of them. If they had seen me they would have killed. But they didn't because I managed to hide. I ran from the army. those goons. they threw grenades at me in the gully. I ran to another ditch like doves flying when they look for a nesting place. They captured 5 in the ambush I was in. I don't have nothing, nothing. Why am I going to lie? We're all poor (potrecitos) In this war we're in we don't win anything. I counted soldiers — they pulled with knives. I'm afraid of the soldiers. Listen, until I scrambled up the hill to hide, the machine gun roared. They shot three bursts at me. They couldn't find me where I hid in the hole I found. [Informe Juiguar / Acatan] Abunda, 54 yrs from ___.

I left the town in terror. But I didn't understand. I felt clean. I've done nothing wrong in my life. I couldn't

**[Notebook 5 — "14:16"]**

roof and flaps on side. "We're prepared to make revolution at whatever cost. No backing down. Sone war is keeping us from moving forward."

The fiesta began about 7:30 pm. Arena mortars & machine gun opened up from our positions at La Virgen towards contra positions at Cerro El Saino. Tracers like roman candle. evangelicals off to side were chanting prayers.

5.23 - 6 am on top Cerro El Saino. 1 contra body, contorted, dropped by mortar. Further ahead, blood on trail. Contras divided into 3 groups to flee. At dawning on top, rushed to recover contra materiel. 3 hats - Regalio. At least there are 3 contras into hats. Reagan said he cut off aid. 1 Spanish G-3 with blood on it, jammed from hot key shrapnel. Canteen belts. Hand grenades. US-made canteens & ammo belts.

Por eso que somos invencibles. dejo Sandino. Talavera.
Contras don't want to fight. Realize they're losing. 2 yrs ago were willing to fight still thought they could take Jinotega, Matagalpa, and move on

**[Notebook 6 — "4:73"]**

I see my role as a priest but also has part of the struggle. In the ideological aspect, it's up to me to orient the people toward a commitment with the people, based on the Word of God. But I consider myself a participant in this struggle. For the people it's important that a priest walks with them, with the same fear but among them. That sometimes we have to run like hell and hide because the airplanes are coming. That I tremble when something happens. But that I am there in the midst of them, suffering the same. maintaining ~~~ optimism and Christian hope. Never have I carried an arm. So that it's ~~~ - I'm here representing the g's (biblical) and to facilitate the coming together of the people. We are few the priests walking with the g's. Unfortunately, we haven't been able to get together.

For me, the priests collaborating with the g's are showing their real face because these people always said "as priests and church we can't take sides. we have to be neutral" But suddenly they appear as members of for. Ex.

**[Notebook 7 — "23"]**

E Bermudez - can move into Nica. Until they hold some territory. 24 Everybody's a contra in Chontales. If I were them I'd head for "Region of maximum acceptability for contras. Can't really take anything on AC until they can neutralize helicopters. Neutralize forward-basing of aircraft. They'd have to spend everything defending against helicopters. Infiltration routes around Salient) but can get in further east. That won't be waging g war. Sandinistas want to prevent resurgence of so. front. Having some success. Problem in south & Chontales - only 1 successful airdrop since Hasenfus went down. Running out of stuff. So. Front - 600. 1 section J. Salazar (3-400 south of Rama road) FDN never has managed to absorb them. Command-control not good. Commanders think. No people. In Chontales you get fed. Down there no food unless you go to towns & if you do that, you're dog meat for Sandinistas. Chontales - presents most opportunities - friendly population, mil. targets. Takes 45 days from A to get down there. May want to start doing something around Apanas.

**[Notebook 8 — "17 / 75"]**

grenades & a divers mask the bug has 2 huge luminescent eyes. We're front line of defense: No other troops between us & border. Up to 300-400 contras could move in here before splitting up in this area. Eery feeling to these woods. Last army troops passed through here 4 mos ago. Great time & laughs grabbing these bugs but knowing gunfire could break out any second. en prenda - viene el prenda during guerrillas have nothing to do in mountains but invent things, think. That's why they're so vivos. But will smoke if you give him a cig. - J

5.1 EN MARCHA: Muerto de cansancio
We're now on top of hill cleared by contras - a landing zone large enough to accommodate a Chinook about 50 km from border.
* Many US Army artifacts - backpacks, cartridge belts, canteens, boots recovered from the contras. Army looks more like a guerrilla army than a regular force. (May 68

**[Notebook 9 — "19 16"]**

Vice-Minister of Defense Joaquin Cuadra, head of General Staff. declarations in Segovia, Dec 1985: 19 16

"strategic defeat" - less possibility of seizing important territory, holding it, and creating platform for greater aggression.
+ Contra activity in strategic Regions I and VI on decline with no chance of recuperating. + No chance of ranks growing numerically. + Population in zone receiving more gov't attention & Resettlements - good lands, technical assistance, health, security, etc. + Social base for contras in zone lost. + Elite forces of contras now based in Honduras. Enter only to strike but they must leave. they can't remain inside. More & more difficult to infiltrate into territory. + Revolutionary forces establishing & stabilizing controls over territory. Ever greater social, political, military reordering favorable to rev.
+ CIA trying to change tactics & theatre of operations. Northern Region V, enemy seeking to create greater forces. Problem of distance from support bases in Honduras.
+ In order to justify Cont'd supports

**[Notebook 10 — "2327"]**

FROM TAPE: (start)

investigations that Nica authorities making re: contra supplies. Hasenfus says Max Gomez was head of supply operation and responsible for coordination with Salvadoran authorities. Took charge also of obtaining I.D for all members of supply team. Hasen. has said that it was known among team + Gomez was friend of V.P Bush. Cooper had certain fear of Gomez b/c he was a man of the CIA. Nica authorities know MG is false name and his true I.D is another. NYT identifies M. Gomez as Felix Rodriguez, CIA advisor who was in Bolivia participating in interrogation of Che Guevara. A person of these same characteristics was acting during 83-84 as rep of CIA before C/R forces of FDN in Honduras. In this case, under name Gustavo Villoldo, also of Cuban origin who had participated in anti-guerrilla ops in Bolivia against Che J, as part of CIA. In 84, group of contra heads sent letter to US Emb to Col. Raymond about request for operational advisor. In letter we have C/R heads requested "possibility of incorporating operationally, in our project Mr. G. Villoldo, who has been very important factor in crisis which recently occurred (letter date Jan. 23. 1984)

of Afghanistan. We're gathered in
a circle in shade of the tree
with Naweed translating in
the middle. Portraits of villagers.
They grow wheat and tend goats.
Wheat harvested 1 months ago. The
man I just photographed says
"Americans can really help us by
making a well. We carry water
by donkeys from very far."
His hair flecked with gray. Padsha.
Now we're hearing gunfire rolling in
from northeast - artillery. Mortars
from border area, about 2-3 k
away. Apparently border dispute
between... Yesterday we were only
1 km from Pakistan. Battallion
commander issued directive to stay
1k back, to keep us away from the
NWO border (there's also the Durant
border, and one other). [ROLL #18]
Portraits. One villager says: we
don't understand what the Americans
are doing. They used to support the
Taliban when the Russians were
here, then they turned against
them." Sean says the villagers just

they're looking for. Steele
says source ID'ed the guy as
participant in an attack on
a coalition convoy 1 months
ago. Meanwhile outside Iraqi
policeman shooting, rifle
pointed at rooftop. A guy
with hands stretched up
is caught in beam of flashlight & the sights of policeman's rifle.
We get back in cars, looks
like we're headed to a nearby location to get someone
else. When bursts of gunfire
ring out from nearby. Steele
pulls car over. We scramble
for cover behind it. After
a few moments, Steele says
"Those are US forces." He
comes out yelling to the
soldiers. They opened fire on
our vehicles. No word if

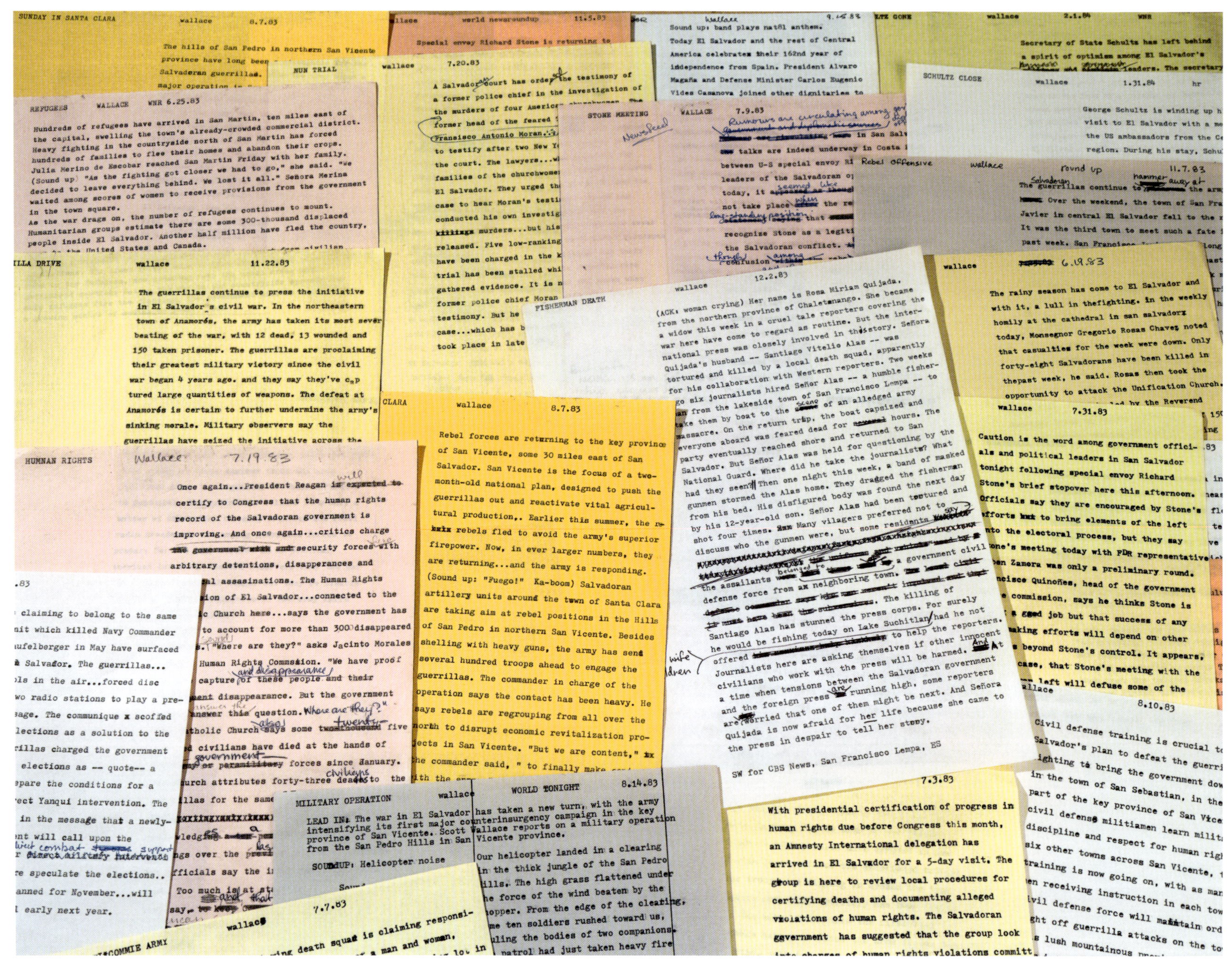


SUNDAY IN SANTA CLARA    wallace    8.7.83
The hills of San Pedro in northern San Vicente province have long been
Salvadoran guerrillas.
major operation in

REFUGES    WALLACE    WNR 6.25.83
Hundreds of refugees have arrived in San Martin, ten miles east of
the capital, swelling the town's already-crowded commercial district.
Heavy fighting in the countryside north of San Martin has forced
hundreds of families to flee their homes and abandon their crops.
Julia Merino de Escobar reached San Martin Friday with her family.
(Sound up) "As the fighting got closer we had to go," she said. "We
decided to leave everything behind. We lost it all." Señora Merina
waited among scores of women to receive provisions from the government
in the town square.
As the war drags on, the number of refugees continues to mount.
Humanitarian groups estimate there are some 300-thousand displaced
people inside El Salvador. Another half million have fled the country,
the United States and Canada.

NUN TRIAL
wallace    7.20.83
A Salvador court has ordered the testimony of
a former police chief in the investigation of
the murders of four American churchwomen
former head of the feared
Francisco Antonio Moran
to testify after two New Y
the court. The lawyers...w
families of the churchwomen
El Salvador. They urged th
case to hear Moran's testi
conducted his own investiga
killings murders...but his
released. Five low-ranking
have been charged in the k
trial has been stalled sin
gathered evidence. It is no
former police chief Moran
testimony. But he
case...which has b
took place in late

WALLACE    7.9.83
Rumors are circulating among
in San Sal
talks are indeed underway in Costa
between U-S special envoy Ri
leaders of the Salvadoran op
today, it seemed like
not take place after the re
recognize Stone as a legiti
the Salvadoran conflict.
confusion among

GUERRILLA DRIVE    wallace    11.22.83
The guerrillas continue to press the initiative
in El Salvador's civil war. In the northeastern
town of Anamorós, the army has taken its most severe
beating of the war, with 12 dead, 13 wounded and
150 taken prisoner. The guerrillas are proclaiming
their greatest military victory since the civil
war began 4 years ago. And they say they've cap
tured large quantities of weapons. The defeat at
Anamorós is certain to further undermine the army's
sinking morale. Military observers say the
guerrillas have seized the initiative across the

HUMAN RIGHTS    Wallace    7.19.83
Once again...President Reagan is expected to will
certify to Congress that the human rights
record of the Salvadoran government is
improving. And once again...critics charge
the government and security forces with
arbitrary detentions, disappearances and
assassinations. The Human Rights
of El Salvador...connected to the
Church here...says the government has
to account for more than 3000 disappeared
"Where are they?" asks Jacinto Morales
Human Rights Commission. "We have proof
capture of these people and their
disappearance. But the government
answer this question. Where are they?"
Church says some two thousand five
civilians have died at the hands of
government paramilitary forces since January.
Church attributes forty-three deaths to the

CLARA    wallace    8.7.83
Rebel forces are returning to the key province
of San Vicente, some 30 miles east of San
Salvador. San Vicente is the focus of a two-
month-old national plan, designed to push the
guerrillas out and reactivate vital agricultural production. Earlier this summer, the re
bels rebels fled to avoid the army's superior
firepower. Now, in ever larger numbers, they
are returning...and the army is responding.
(Sound up: "Fuego!" Ka-boom) Salvadoran
artillery units around the town of Santa Clara
are taking aim at rebel positions in the Hills
of San Pedro in northern San Vicente. Besides
shelling with heavy guns, the army has sent
several hundred troops ahead to engage the
guerrillas. The commander in charge of the
operation says the contact has been heavy. He
says rebels are regrouping from all over the
north to disrupt economic revitalization projects in San Vicente. "But we are content,"
the commander said, " to finally make

FISHERMAN DEATH
wallace    12.2.83
(ACK, woman crying) Her name is Rosa Miriam Quijada,
from the northern province of Chalatenango. She became
a widow this week in a cruel tale reporters covering the
war here have come to regard as routine. But the international press was closely involved in this story. Señora
Quijada's husband -- Santiago Vitelio Alas -- was
tortured and killed by a local death squad, apparently
for his collaboration with Western reporters. Two weeks
ago six journalists hired Señor Alas -- a humble fisherman from the lakeside town of San Francisco Lempa -- to
take them by boat to the scene of an alleged army
massacre. On the return trip, the boat capsized and
everyone aboard was feared dead for hours. The
party eventually reached shore and returned to San
Salvador. But Señor Alas was held for questioning by the
National Guard. Where did he take the journalists? What
had they seen? Then one night this week, a band of masked
gunmen stormed the Alas home. They dragged the fisherman
from his bed. His disfigured body was found the next day
by his 12-year-old son. Señor Alas had been tortured and
shot four times. Many villagers preferred not to
discuss who the gunmen were, but some residents
the assailants belonged to a government civil
defense force from a neighboring town. The killing of
Santiago Alas has stunned the press corps. For surely
he would be fishing today on Lake Suchitlan had he not
offered to help the reporters.
Journalists here are asking themselves if other innocent
civilians who work with the press will be harmed. At
a time when tensions between the Salvadoran government
and the foreign press are running high, some reporters
are worried that one of them might be next. And Señora
Quijada is now afraid for her life because she came to
the press in despair to tell her story.
SW for CBS News, San Francisco Lempa, ES

wallace    6.19.83
The rainy season has come to El Salvador and
with it, a lull in the fighting. In the weekly
homily at the cathedral in San Salvador
today, Monsenor Gregorio Rosas Chavez noted
that casualties for the week were down. Only
forty-eight Salvadorans have been killed in
the past week, he said. Rosas then took the
opportunity to attack the Unification Church.

wallace    7.31.83
Caution is the word among government officials and political leaders in San Salvador
tonight following special envoy Richard
Stone's brief stopover here this afternoon.
Officials say they are encouraged by Stone's
efforts but to bring elements of the left
into the electoral process, but they say
Stone's meeting today with FDR representative
Ruben Zamora was only a preliminary round.
Francisco Quinones, head of the government
peace commission, says he thinks Stone is
doing a good job but that success of any
peacemaking efforts will depend on other
factors beyond Stone's control. It appears,
in any case, that Stone's meeting with the
left will defuse some of the

wallace    8.10.83
Civil defense training is crucial to
Salvador's plan to defeat the guerri
fighting to bring the government dow
in the town of San Sebastian, in the
part of the key province of San Vice
civil defense militiamen learn milit
discipline and respect for human rig
six other towns across San Vicente,
training is now going on, with as man
receiving instruction in each town
civil defense force will maintain ord
fight off guerrilla attacks on the to
lush mountainous

claiming to belong to the same
unit which killed Navy Commander
Schaufelberger in May have surfaced
Salvador. The guerrillas...
in the air...forced disc
two radio stations to play a pre-
message. The communique scoffed
elections as a solution to the
guerrillas charged the government
elections as -- quote-- a
prepare the conditions for a
direct Yanqui intervention. The
in the message that a newly-
will call upon the
which combat support
foreign military intervention
speculate the elections..
planned for November...will
early next year.
COMMIE ARMY

MILITARY OPERATION    wallace    8.14.83
LEAD IN: The war in El Salvador has taken a new turn, with the army
intensifying its first major counterinsurgency campaign in the key
province of San Vicente. Scott Wallace reports on a military operation
from the San Pedro Hills in San Vicente province.
SOUNDUP: Helicopter noise
Sound
7.7.83
wallace

WORLD TONIGHT    wallace    7.3.83
Our helicopter landed in a clearing
in the thick jungle of the San Pedro
Hills. The high grass flattened under
the force of the wind beaten by the
chopper. From the edge of the clearing,
some ten soldiers rushed toward us,
hauling the bodies of two companions.
The patrol had just taken heavy fire
death squad is claiming responsi-
a man and woman,

With presidential certification of progress in
human rights due before Congress this month,
an Amnesty International delegation has
arrived in El Salvador for a 5-day visit. The
group is here to review local procedures for
certifying deaths and documenting alleged
violations of human rights. The Salvadoran
government has suggested that the group look
into charges of human rights violations committ

world newsroundup    11.5.83
Special envoy Richard Stone is returning to

Sound up; band plays nat'l anthem.
wallace    9.15.83
Today El Salvador and the rest of Central
America celebrates their 162nd year of
independence from Spain. President Alvaro
Magaña and Defense Minister Carlos Eugenio
Vides Casanova joined other dignitaries to

LATE GONE    wallace    2.1.84    WNR
Secretary of State Schultz has left behind
a spirit of optimism among El Salvador's
leaders. The secretary

SCHULTZ CLOSE    wallace    1.31.84    hr
George Schultz is winding up his
visit to El Salvador with a me
the US ambassadors from the Ce
region. During his stay, Schu

Rebel Offensive    wallace    round up    11.7.83
The guerrillas continue to hammer away at
Over the weekend, the town of San Fra
Javier in central El Salvador fell to the r
It was the third town to meet such a fate
past week. San Francisco

8.13.83

The hills of San Pedro in northern San
Vicente province offer some of the roughest
terrain in all of El Salvador. Until
recently, they were a major guerrilla
stronghold. But the government, with advice
from U.S. military experts, launched a
offensive across San Vicente in June. Army
patrols now penetrate the jungle, hacking
their way through the dense underbrush. (SU)
With special counterinsurgency
training from the American advisers, a new
breed of Salvadoran soldier stalks the valley
and mountains of San Vicente. The soldier
stay off the beaten tra...
guerril...

Abriendo
brecha

(ACK: woman crying) Her name is Rosa Miriam Quijada,
the northern province of Chaletenango. She became
ow this week in a cruel tale reporters covering the
ere have come to regard as routine. But th...
nal press was closely invol...
da's husb...

Salvadoran
offensive     wallace

SANTA CLARA     wallace

LEAD IN: El Salvador remains the key factor in the Central American
And in El Salvador, the US-backed government is palcing most of its
on a province called San Vicente. Scott Wallace reports from one
torn area.

When night falls on Santa Clara, you can only
hear the barking of stray dogs. Like hundreds
of twons across El Salvador, Santa Clara is
a mere shadow of its past. Most of the town's
people pulled out a long ago, their abandoned
homes since occupied by refugees from smaller
villages. Soldiers sleep on tables in the
marketplace where townfolk one gathered until
the morning hours. The electricity is often
out in Santa Clara, and those who venture into
the streets must rely on dim light from the
moon for guidance. Throughout the night, the
calm is shattered by bursts
of gunfire from the surrounding hills as small
guerrilla bands move in to harrass the
soldiers guarding the town. As long as the
army remains, the guerrillas aren't likely to
launch a major attack. But noone here forgets
that the rebels are just a few miles away.

wallace     9.16.83

PARRAXTUT     GUATEMALA SERIES # 3     wallace     9.16.83

Parraxtut is wind-swept town, remotely set on a
mountain top in the highlands of western Guatemala.
You have to look beyond the appearance of this
poverty-stricken town, with its mixture of adobe
huts and tin-roofed shacks, to understand the
sadness of its people and their reluctance to talk
with strangers. For here in Parraxtut...some time
last year...one of the biggest massacres in Central
America's recent history is said to have occurred.
According to villagers in Parraxtut, some two-
hundred-fifty people -- mostly women, children
and elderly -- were killed and many of the town's
houses burned down. Scattered among the traditional
stucco huts, newer tin-roofed hovels provide a
clue to Parraxtut's recent nightmare.
These newly-constructed shacks mark the spot where
the older ones burned. An eery stillness prevails
in the cemetery above the town. Across a stretch
of several yards lies a mass grave large enough
to hold scores of bodies. In what must have been
a hasty job, no markers were left to identify the
victims. An army officer said the guerrillas swept
down on Parraxtut to seek revenge for the loss of
popular support among the town's people. But
villagers repeated in an uneasy whisper that it
was the army that came to burn the town and kill
its people. As in hundreds of towns across
western Guatemala, confusion remains. The people
swear they saw the army do it. The army says it
was the guerrillas dressed in uniforms, disguised

8.10.83

...e lies in the heart of El Salvador's
...ltural belt, strategically located
...n Salvador and the eastern
...Both the Salvadoran army and rebel
...San Vicente as a crucial area,
...ar for El Salvador may be won or
...rmy launched a major offensive from base
...to drive guerrillas from base
...ld throughout the province. The
...s now trying to resettle refugees
...store desperately-needed
...tion. The combined military
...ci-... n is also aimed at
...rovince's shattered infra-
... communication lines.
...s. After a two month lull,
... now returning to the
...r clashes between the army
... reported throughout the
...e past week. With govern-
...ull swing and guerrillas
...e tide in the war, the
... San Vicente, and
...w underway.

...an Vicente, El Salvador

secretary shyed away from strong language
concerning the sticky question of human
rights. He condemned both death squad violence
and what he called "totalitarian terror,"
referring to the violent tactics of the
rebels. Schultz is now meeting with top
civilian and military leaders and will
...with US ambassadors from all over

round up     hammer away at

The guerrillas continue to ... the army.

Over the weekend, the town of San Fransisco
Javier in central El Salvador fell to the rebels.
It was the third town to meet such a fate in the
past week. San Francisco Javier lies along a
strategic corridor through central and eastern
El Salvador where the reb...

11.7.83     world newsroundup     11.5.83

Special envoy Richard Stone is returning to
El Salvador today to pursue, in the words of
a State Department official, his mission of
attaining a dialogue between the Salvadoran
government and the leftist opposition.

10.26.83     wallace

This is Scott Wallace in Usulutan Province,
El Salvador.

I came across the guerrillas as the sun set on
the river. In the hazy twilight some thirty young
men glided across the river on a raft. They all
carried automatic weapons. Their crossing took
them past the twisted wreckage of a steel bridge.
It once linked the provincial capital to the
cotton fields of Jucuaran. Two years ago, the
guerrillas blew it up. The rebles now climbed the
riverbank and assembled on the dirt road. The
strategic coastal highway was only four miles
away. Each man had a different uniform -- maybe
a straw hat, a t-shirt or a pair of combat
fatigues. They all belonged to the Zablah brigade,
a crack regiment of Salvadoran guerrillas. They
spoke with confidence about their cause and their
determination to win. Their morale seems high.
They say the army fears them and stays away. The
rebels insist most their weapons come from the
United States. They claim to have captured nearly
400 U.S.-supplied weapons from the army in the
past two months.

As darkness fell, the guerrillas moved up the
road toward the coastal highway.

It can often happen in this part of El Salvador.
I came across the guerrillas by chance, leaving
the highway for a backroad. I hadn't seen a
single soldier for miles. The guerrillas say they
control this long stretch of cotton fields and
fishing towns. The army is spread too thin
elsewhere, they say, to try to take it back.

SW for CBS News, Usulutan Province, El Salvador

WNR 1.31.84

When Secretary of State George Schultz arrives
here later this
morning, he'll encounter a host of military
and government officials anxious to express
their enthusiasm for President Reagan's plan
to increase aid for El Salvador. Schultz will
spend the morning conducting high-level
talks with Salvadoran president Alvaro
Magana and Defense Minister General Vides Casanova.
The secretary will confer later with the
heads of the political parties running in
the coming elections. Local businessmen and
government officials are optimistic the
recently-released
Kissinger Commission report will sway Congress
on Central America
toward greater support for the administration
efforts to defeat the rebels here. The
rebels scoff at Schultz's visit. They charge the
U.S. with offering only war to the people of
El Salvador. They say Schultz will bring no
constructive solutions...

violence that has racked El Salvador for the last
four years. Cancel's husband, Curtis Lewenz, says
the couple thought they'd be safe traveling through
El Salvador, despite the civil war here.
embassy officials here say the death of Linda
Cancel should be a reminder to other travelers that
El Salvador isn't a place  It was too late
before Lewenz realized their faith in God would not
be enough to guarantee the safety of his family
or the fulfillment of their dreams of living
together  protect this dreams of
peaceful life together in the neighboring

The hills of San Pedro in northern San Vicente
province have long been a stronghold for the
Salvadoran guerrillas.
When the army began a
Vicente two months ago,
t, giving the province
e rebels are back, and

...the past 18 months, the G...
has conducted a broad counter...
campaign in the country's we...
They call the program "Bulle...
The bullets refer to securit...
guerillas into isolated, shr...
The beans mean food for theu...
uprooted by the violence plus
roads, schools and cli...

GUATEMALAN SERIES # 4     wallace     9.16.8...

The Ixil triangle in northwestern Gu...
one of the most strife-torn re...
entire
country. ...
army officer assigned to the area c...
triangle the most affected by Marxi...
- quote -
subversion in all of Guatemala. The...
of people living here are "indigen...
who speak the Ixil language. Guerr...
operating here by the end of the 1...
willing recruits among the Indians...
had long been neglected by Guatema...
rulers. Fighting still rages in th...
mountainous region. The Guatemala...
"continuous offensive" against th...
began 18 months ago.  Besides di...
guerrilla forces, the army's
the rebels from the local Ixil p...
the army still suspects of colla...
guerrillas. This strategy has
refugees who continue...
to stream in from the moun...
the larger towns. Army officers
Mao Zedong's addage: ... civ...
guerrillas as the sea is to fish...
removal of civilians from their
to draining the sea, leaving th...
and gasping for air. T...
Indians are really fleeing the
ceived them with promises of
radise. But many refugees sa...

them to write ...
they see or think. The Monsignore sa...
anyone who wants to find out about...
really going on in El Salvador mus...
outside publications or broadcast...
says Salvadoran journalists must
themselves or risk being fired b...
ideological employers. The Mons...
concluded his tribute to the j...
telling them -- quote -- peace
cannot be constucted on lies.

Scott Wallace (top center, third from the right with hands on hips) joins a press conference in San Salvador, El Salvador, 1984. Photograph © Robert Nickelsberg and used with permission.

*Acronyms*

ARENA: Nationalist Republican Alliance (El Salvador)

BLI: Irregular Warfare Battalion (Nicaragua)

BRAZ: Rafael Arce Zablah Brigade of the ERP (El Salvador)

CIA: Central Intelligence Agency (U.S.A.)

EPS: Ejército Popular Sandinista or Sandinista Popular Army, sometimes referred to as simply the Sandinista Army (Nicaragua)

ERP: People's Revolutionary Army (El Salvador)*

FMLN: Farabundo Martí National Liberation Front (El Salvador)

FPL: Popular Liberation Forces, (El Salvador)*

FSLN: Sandinista National Liberation Front (Nicaragua)

PCN: National Conciliation Party (El Salvador)

* One of the FMLN's five rebel armies

Endsheets: Scott Wallace's two montages present headlines from his articles on Central America that appeared from 1983 to 1990 in *The Atlanta Journal-Constitution*, *The Guardian*, *The Independent*, *The Nation*, and *Newsweek*.

2: Sandinista Popular Army troops uproot peasant families in the deep countryside to create a "free-fire zone" to battle the Contra rebels, El Ventarrón, Nicaragua, February 1985. The Sandinista Popular Army (EPS), sometimes referred to as the Sandinista Army, was the national army of Nicaragua during the years of rule (1979–1990) by the Sandinista National Liberation Front (FSLN).

4: Jesús Cartagena recounts the harrowing details of a massacre allegedly committed days before by soldiers of the U.S.-trained Atlatcatl battalion, rebel-held Chalatenango, El Salvador, September 1984.

6: Rebels of the FMLN enter the city of Chinameca while on offensive across eastern El Salvador, October 1983.

11: Women gather in Managua to protest U.S. support for the Contra rebels, holding photographs of loved ones killed in Contra attacks in the north and central war zones of Nicaragua, June 1987.

14: Bill Gentile's photograph was made in April 1984.

20L: Casper Weinberger's press conference was held in September 1983.

20R: Also pictured with Jeane Kirkpatrick is General Adolfo Blandón (left), Salvadoran Army Chief of Staff, April 1985.

21: Henry Kissinger, appointed by President Ronald Reagan to lead the National Bipartisan Commission on Central

America, arrives in San Salvador with other members of the commission, October 1983. Kissinger is flanked by U.S. Ambassador Thomas Pickering (left of Kissinger, in the dark suit) and Salvadoran Foreign Minister Fidel Chávez Mena (right of Kissinger, in the light suit.)

22L: Scott Wallace interviews government soldiers guarding a bridge on the Pan-American Highway, July 1983. Photograph by William Clary, taken on Scott Wallace's camera.

22R: Photojournalists bide time while awaiting help to pull their vehicle (with a TV taped to the windows) from high water at a river crossing, Estelí Department, Nicaragua, April 1984.

23: Scott Wallace with CBS sound tech Jaime Robles (fourth from the left) and Reuters correspondent Bobby Block (center, with mustache) with guerrilla escorts after crossing the Sumpul River on their way to investigate charges of a government army massacre of leftist peasants, known as *masas*, rebel-held Chalatenango Department, September 1984. Photograph by Roberto Pineda, taken on Scott Wallace's camera.

24: A boy joins a street demonstration against abductions and disappearances of labor leaders and other suspected leftists by death squads linked to government security forces, June 1983.

27: A prisoner implicated in the killings of twelve peasants is brought to the site of the murders while family members of the victims look on, April 1984. The man was a member of a local Civil Defense unit involved in murdering the victims and throwing them to the bottom of a 180-foot well, Los Mangos, Sonsonate Department.

28: A government army officer applies camouflage paint to his face using a makeup compact at the start of an operation against leftist guerrillas, Santa Elena, Usulután Department, March 1984.

29: A member of the peasant militia of the FPL hoists his Belgian-made FAL rifle in the guerrilla-controlled hamlet of El Zapotal, Chalatenango Department, October 1984. The militia were assigned to protect civilians in the guerrillas' rear guard territories.

30: Belgian-born revolutionary priest Rogelio Ponseele (left) accompanies leftist guerrillas from the FMLN, Jucuarán, Usulután Department, October 1983. The controversial cleric gave up his parish duties for a life on the run with the rebels in 1980 after several members of his congregation were killed by death squads linked to the government.

31: Revelers show off their disguises during annual carnival celebrations in the war-torn town of Estanzuelas, Usulután Department, June 1984.

32: Indigenous members of the Civil Defense patrol in traditional dress march along a mountainside outside Todos Santos Cuchumatán, Huehuetenango Department, September 1983. Guatemala's military government kept a tight inventory on weapons issued to the patrols, as evidenced by the numbers painted on the rifle stocks shown here.

33: Three generations—including a grandfather (left, in the background with a team of yoked oxen), father, and daughter—produce and package sugar at a *trapiche*, a traditional sugar mill, Uspantán, El Quiché Department, September 1983.

34: Lieutenant Colonel Domingo Monterrosa and Colonel Mauricio Staben brief troops at the start of an army operation to clear rebels in advance of national elections, Santa Elena, Usulután Department, March 1984. Monterrosa would be killed in October 1984, when FMLN rebels detonated a remote-controlled bomb in his helicopter over the mountains of Morazán.

35: Salvadoran President José Napoleón Duarte leaves funeral services for Lieutenant Colonel Domingo Monterrosa, flanked by Army Chief of Staff General Adolfo Blandón (left) and Defense Minister General Carlos Eugenio Vides Casanova (right), October 1984.

36: Human remains lie with a baby bottle in the aftermath of an alleged massacre of civilian supporters of the guerrillas by the U.S.-trained Atlacatl Battalion, Gualsinga River, September 1984.

37: Lady guerrillas of the FMLN on New Year's Day, Tenancingo, Cuscatlán Department, January 1985.

38: Peasants take a break from their labors in the rebel-controlled hamlet of El Zapotal, Chalatenango Department, September 1984.

39: Villagers tend to a young woman gravely wounded in a clash between government army troops and FMLN rebels in advance of national elections, Las Marías, Usulután Department, March 1984.

40: Rosa Miriam Quijada de Alas (left), with her family of orphaned children, San Francisco Lempa, Chalatenango Department, El Salvador, December 1983. Her husband, Santiago Vitelio Alas, was abducted and murdered the night before this image was made by a local death squad after he took foreign journalists in his boat down Lake Suchitlán to the scene of an alleged massacre committed by the Salvadoran Army. (Also see my telexed report of this story on page 158.)

41: National Guardmen check voter IDs as polls open in national elections, Jiquilisco, Usulután Department, March 1989.

42: Pro-Sandinista peasants armed with AK-47s stand guard at a state-run "auto-defense cooperative," September 1986. The Sandinista government established nearly 3,000 such fortified farms, which were crucial in keeping strategic thoroughfares open in the countryside while serving as firebases for heavy artillery.

43: Volunteer *brigadistas* receive a security briefing before they head into the coffee groves to start the day's harvest at a state-run farm, Finca La Sorpresa, Jinotega Department, February 1986.

44: An Indigenous bride and groom walk in their wedding procession through the streets of San Juan Cotzal, El Quiché Department, July 1989.

45: A twelve-year-old guerrilla brandishes his M-16 rifle during a lull in fighting with government army forces, Election Day, San Francisco Javier, Usulután Department, March 1989.

46: The conductor leads a military band and honor guard at funeral services for an assassinated rightwing legislator, June 1983.

49T: Workers stencil the initials of the PCN on a rock face during the run-up to national elections, February 1984. The PCN was the official party of the military governments that ruled El Salvador throughout the 1960s and 1970s. By the 1980s, its influence among the military and land-owning elite was eclipsed by the extreme-right ARENA.

49B: Interim President Alvaro Magaña and Roberto d'Aubuisson, President of the Legislative Assembly and alleged death-squad leader, at the funeral ceremony for a slain rightwing legislator, National Assembly, June 1983.

51: Mourners gather outside the Metropolitan Cathedral on the fifth anniversary of the death of Archbishop Óscar Arnulfo Romero, March 1985. The assassination of Romero by a death-squad sniper in 1980 marked the beginning of El Salvador's twelve-year civil war. Canonized a saint by Pope Francis in 2018, Romero was a vocal critic of government repression.

53: Cadets at a graduation ceremony at Captain General Gerardo Barrios Military School, the Salvadoran military's elite officer-training academy, in San Salvador, El Salvador, July 1983.

54: Women march in downtown San Salvador to protest political kidnappings and disappearances of loved ones at the hands of security forces and death squads, June 1983.

56: Soldiers of a U.S.-trained "hunter battalion" during a search-and-destroy sweep in search of leftist rebels, San Pedro Hills, San Vicente Department, July 1983.

58: Residents rebuild their war-ravaged town with wages paid by U.S. economic aid, San Lorenzo, San Vicente Department, El Salvador, July 1983.

61L: A drill sergeant (center right) barks orders to recently drafted recruits being formed into "hunter battalions" to press the offensive against leftist rebels, July 1983.

61R: Mourners walk in a funeral procession for relatives killed in recent fighting between government forces and leftist rebels, July 1983.

63: Soldiers of the U.S.-trained Arce Battalion fan out across parched fields on an operation to push rebels out of the area in advance of national elections, Las Marías, Usulután Department, March 1984.

64: Members of a Mayan Indigenous Civil Defense patrol stand guard at a roadblock, Todos Santos Cuchumatán, Huehuetenango Department, Western Highlands, September 1983.

67: Members of an Indigenous Civil Defense patrol share a light moment, as one *patrullero* displays a hand grenade, September 1983.

68: Soldiers of the Guatemalan Army, armed with Israeli-made Galil assault rifles, take up positions at a frontline outpost in the Ixil Region, El Quiché Department, September 1983. The Guatemalan military was found by international investigators to have committed hundreds of massacres of Indigenous Maya during the war, which formally ended in 1996.

71: An Indigenous Ixil girl and her brother wait at the window of a corner shop in the early morning, San Juan Cotzal, El Quiché Department, September 1983.

73: Indigenous Maya children line up to receive provisions at the Río Azul "model village," Nebaj, Ixil Region, El Quiché Department, Guatemala, September 1983. After razing Native communities suspected of collaborating with leftist guerrillas in a scorched-earth campaign that left tens of thousands dead, the Guatemalan military resettled surviving Maya in concentrated villages such as this one.

74: Rebels belonging to the FMLN's battle-hardened BRAZ unit pose for a photograph alongside a cable-guided ferry, Río Grande de San Miguel, La Anchila, Usulután Department, October 1983. The 1,000-member brigade won grudging admiration from U.S. military advisors for its prowess in combat against the government army.

77: Government army soldiers check IDs and frisk passengers on a bus heading from the city of San Miguel to San Salvador, Coastal Highway, Usulután Department, El Salvador, March 1984.

79: Peasant members of the ERP patrol the road to Perquín in rebel-controlled Morazán Department, El Salvador, May 1984. The ERP was the largest of the rebel armies operating in eastern El Salvador.

80T: Local peasants help load the CBS News van aboard a ferry to cross the Río Grande de San Miguel in order to reach the rebel-controlled town of Jucuarán, Usulután Department, October 1983.

80B: CBS News correspondent Mike O'Connor (center) and cameraman Dan Riesenfeld (right) interview an FMLN guerrilla commander (left, with rifle), La Anchila, Usulután Department, October 1983.

82: Women and children recall their harrowing tale of surviving an alleged massacre by the Salvadoran Army in which fifty peasant supporters of the FMLN guerrillas were reported to have died, rebel-held Chalatenango Department, September 1984.

85: A guerrilla of the FPL holds an armadillo as he prepares to join a train of horses and mules to resupply encampments deep in the mountains of rebel-held Chalatenango Department, El Salvador, September 1984. The FPL operated throughout northern and central El Salvador.

87: Reuters correspondent Bobby Block (center, drinking from a canteen) and CBS News cameraman Roberto Pineda (right) with guerrilla escorts after crossing a dilapidated footbridge spanning the rain-swollen Sumpul River, Chalatenango, El Salvador, September 1984.

89: Mourners wail at the funeral for relatives in the local Civil Defense killed in a rebel attack, Santa Cruz Loma, La Paz Department, April 1985.

90L: A guerrilla couple celebrates the New Year in the town of Tenancingo, Cuscatlán Department, January 1985.

90R: A young girl leans against a graffiti-dappled house, September 1984. The graffiti pays tribute to "Comandante Ana María," Mélida Anaya Montes, a co-founder of the FPL. She was assassinated in an internecine dispute at a rebel safe house in Managua in 1983.

92: Soldiers of the elite Santos López BLI of the Sandinista Army cross a burned field while on an operation in search of Contra rebels, June 1985.

95: In a show of distain for the Sandinista government, Contra rebels burn a copy of *Barricada*, the official Sandinista Front newspaper, Quilalí, Nueva Segovia Department, October 1987.

97: Sandinista Army troops survey the smoldering wreckage of their convoy minutes after they suffered an ambush at the hands of Contra rebels, Santo Tomás, Chontales Department, October 1987. Twenty soldiers were killed and sixteen wounded in the attack.

98T: Military pall bearers carry the casket of Sub-Commander Enrique Schmidt Cuadra through the streets of Managua, November 1984. Schmidt Cuadra, Commander of the Pablo Úbeda special forces of the Interior Ministry, was killed in a firefight with Contras in Nicaragua's Central Highlands days earlier. He was among the highest-ranking Sandinista officials to die at the hands of the Contra rebels during the war.

98B: A convoy of East German trucks transports soldiers of the Sandinista Army along a mountain road, June 1987. Ambushes by Contra rebels on such convoys in northern and central Nicaragua were among the deadliest forms of engagement for Sandinista forces.

100: Lieutenant Noel Talavera (center middle, standing) and two Sandinista Army officers (center left and right) examine the body of a Contra rebel just killed in a clash with the Santos López Irregular Warfare Battalion, Cerro El Saíno, Jinotega Department, June 1985. The Contra was shot dead in an exchange of fire after refusing to surrender.

102: Residents of the Indigenous Miskito hamlet of Haulover on Nicaragua's Atlantic Coast gather for a group photograph, September 1985. The scene of several armed clashes during the Contra War, Haulover was destroyed by Eta and Iota, back-to-back Category 4 hurricanes, in November 2020.

105: Miskito rebel commander Uriel Vanegas meets with Sandinista Comandante and Interior Minister Tomás Borge to announce that he and his 400 Indigenous fighters are ending their five-year war with the Sandinista government, October 1987.

106: Miskito fishermen recline on their fishing nets amid amused youngsters, September 1985.

109: A rainbow on the road to the Atlantic Coast city of Puerto Cabezas, La Rosita, Zelaya Norte, November 1986.

110L: A Miskito rebel honoring the ceasefire with the Sandinista government wears a Pope John Paul II cap while relaxing on a hotel veranda, September 1985.

110R: Miskito preacher Eagle Ignacio stands in front of his home as his wife looks on from the kitchen window, Yulu, Zelaya Norte, November 1986.

112: Elite troops from the Sandinista Army board a Soviet-made Mi-17 helicopter during an air-mobile operation in search of Contra rebels, May 1987.

114: Sandinista Army troops on operation against the Contras pass beneath the stump of a giant ceiba tree (*Ceiba pentandra*) evidently cut by timber poachers, May 1987.

116L: A Sandinista Army lieutenant waits for helicopters to arrive at a landing zone carved from the jungle to extricate his unit, Amaka River Valley, Jinotega Department, May 1987.

116R: Contra rebels stand guard at a home of peasant sympathizers, Quilalí, Nueva Segovia Department, October 1987.

118: A Sandinista Army sergeant presents the author with a monkey head while on operation against Contra rebels, May 1987. "Take it as a gift to your girlfriend in Managua," he said.

119: Sandinista Popular Army recruits horse around before their elite battalion heads into combat against U.S.-backed Contra rebels, April 1987. The soldiers brandish Soviet-made AK-47 assault rifles, the standard-issue weapon of the Sandinista Popular Army.

120: Marlon Ortega (center, with TV camera) is flanked by his sound tech Gustavo and still photographer Oscar Navarette while on operation with the Sandinista Popular Army, May 1987. Marlon and Gustavo were killed days later when their helicopter was shot down by U.S.-backed Contra rebels armed with heat-seeking Redeye missiles.

122: Villagers gawk at the body of a government soldier slain in an Election Day attack by FMLN guerrillas, San Francisco Javier, Usulután Department, March 1989.

125: Guerrillas of the FMLN rest in front of the post office during a lull in Election Day fighting with government forces, San Francisco Javier, Usulután Department, El Salvador, March 1989.

126: Salvadoran Army soldiers take cover on the frontlines, a block from rebel positions during street-to-street fighting, Mejicanos District, San Salvador, November 1989.

129: Anguished visitors to the metropolitan morgue look for missing loved ones among the casualties from fighting between the U.S.-backed government and leftist FMLN rebels, San Salvador, El Salvador, November 1989.

130: During a major offensive on the capital, FMLN rebels stop to listen to nearby gunfire and prepare to withdraw up the street, Mejicanos district, San Salvador, November 1989.

132: Awaiting orders to demobilize, Contra rebels cure raw meat in a cease-fire zone secured by the United Nations, La Piñuela, Zelaya Sur, April 1990.

135: "Vitamina," a Contra fighter who chose the pseudonym because he owned a vitamin store before the war, shows off his crucifix and hand grenades, symbols of his religious faith and political convictions, Quilalí, Nueva Segovia Department, October 1987.

137T: An evangelical preacher leads a prayer session for Contra fighters as they prepare to infiltrate into Nicaragua from their cross-border sanctuary, Yamales, El Paraíso Department, Honduras, August 1989.

137B: Freshly supplied with U.S.-furnished weapons, Contra rebels prepare to infiltrate into Nicaragua from their main base camp, Yamales, El Paraíso Department, Honduras, August 1989.

139: A Sandinista Army soldier displays a bandana in favor of Nicaraguan President Daniel Ortega, who lost to Violeta Barrios de Chamorro, the U.S.-backed opposition candidate, in national elections two weeks earlier, March 1990. Ortega's defeat marked the end of the Contra War as well as the end of the Sandinista revolutionary government that came to power following the overthrow of the Somoza family dictatorship in 1979.

140: A suspected looter is detained by a U.S. Army patrol in Saddam Hussein's former Ministry of Information building, which was bombed out during the early stages of the American-led invasion, July 2003.

143: A defaced and bullet-ridden mosaic of Saddam Hussein hints at the chaos that ensued following the U.S.-led invasion of Iraq, July 2003. Saddam's likeness is seen here painted over with the iconic (and somewhat ironic) Smiley Face.

145: An American soldier scans the street with binoculars at a guard post, July 2003.

146: A mixed patrol of forces from the U.S. Army's 82nd Airborne Division and the Army of Afghanistan marches toward a village near the border of Pakistan in the early morning, June 2003.

148: 1st Sergeant Alec Lazore of the U.S. Army's 1st Armored Division rides in his Humvee through the Mansour district of Baghdad with his pistol drawn, July 2003. Radio codes are scrawled with a grease pencil on the windshield.

150: U.S. Army soldiers display photographs of their wives kept in their helmets while on patrol in the restive city of Fallujah, July 2003.

153: U.S. Army soldiers patrol central Baghdad at twilight, July 2003.

156: Press credential issued to Scott Wallace of CBS News by the High Command of the Armed Forces of El Salvador, predating ID cards, which were later provided to journalists.

157: Credentials issued to Scott Wallace by media organizations, governments, and military authorities in Central America from 1983 to 1990 and by U.S. military authorities in Afghanistan and Iraq in 2003.

158: The first page of Scott Wallace's story for *The Atlanta Journal-Constitution* about the murder of a boatman by a local death squad in San Francisco Lempa, El Salvador, apparently for his collaboration with foreign journalists. Wallace filed his stories to Atlanta via telex (seen in the photo) from the CBS News Bureau in San Salvador, December 1983. (Also see my photo of the boatman's family on page 40.)

160–61: From early in his time in Central America, Scott Wallace took meticulous field notes that would allow him to reconstruct events with convincing detail and authenticity. He later assigned numbers to every page and notebook (seen in the upper-right corner of the pages).

162–63: Radio scripts banged out on a portable Olivetti typewriter by Scott Wallace for broadcast on CBS News Radio. The scripts frequently included a suggested lead-in for the news anchor broadcasting from New York.

164: Scott Wallace joins a press conference as Salvadoran Army spokesman Lieutenant Colonel Ricardo Cienfuegos announces the deaths of Lieutenant Colonel Domingo Monterrosa, three other key army field commanders, and ten additional personnel in a helicopter explosion in Morazán Department, October 1984. Leftist rebels, who blamed Monterrosa for command authority over the 1981 El Mozote massacre in Morazán, disclosed years later that they had placed a remote-controlled bomb aboard the helicopter.

173: A craftsman and his children display theatrical masks used in folkloric dances in the front room of his shop, April 1984. Sandinistas used such masks to conceal their identities during the insurrection that toppled dictator Anastasio Somoza in 1979. The masks were made famous in photographs by Susan Meiselas, the celebrated American documentary photographer.

174: A girl pauses in front of a shop dappled with graffiti in the likeness of Augusto César Sandino, the guerrilla leader who fought U.S. Marines during the 1920s and 1930s and inspired the revolutionary FSLN that governed Nicaragua in the years 1979–1990, March 1990.

180: Members of the Sandinista Popular Militia provide an armed escort for a truck laden with supplies on a volatile road along Nicaragua's border with Honduras, April 1984.

184: Reuters correspondent Bobby Black interviews a FMLN guerrilla commander while investigating allegations of a government army massacre, Chalatenango Department, September 1984. Standing behind him is Jaime Robles, CBS News sound technician.

188: On assignment for *Newsweek,* Scott Wallace speaks with Miskito rebels about the war on Nicaragua's Atlantic Coast, November 1986.

190: Hand-written notes cover Scott Wallace's desk at his home office in Guatemala City, October 1989.

Theatrical masks, Masaya, Nicaragua, 1984.

Street corner, Estelí, Nicaragua, 1990.

Note: Page numbers are provided for newspaper and magazine sources where available.

*Introduction*

1. Stephen G. Rabe, *The Killing Zone: The United States Wages Cold War in Latin America, Second Edition* (New York, N.Y.: Oxford University Press, 2016), 138–42.

2. Col. Joseph Stringham, Military Briefing, U.S. Embassy, San Salvador, unpublished Scott Wallace notes (November 21, 1983).

3. The coups in both countries had snuffed out democratic leftist governments and brought to power tyrannical military dictatorships. Both overthrows were instigated, if not outright orchestrated, by the United States. The 1954 coup in Guatemala, in particular, continued to resonate, undermining the U.S.'s credibility as the guardian of democracy and radicalizing the left throughout Latin America.

4. Guy Gugliotta and Douglas Farah, "12 Years of Tortured Truth on El Salvador," *The Washington Post* (March 21, 1993): A36.

5. Scott Wallace, "You Must Go Home Again: Deported L.A. Gangbangers Take Over El Salvador," *Harper's* (August 2000): 47–56.

6. Peter Kornbluh and Malcolm Byrne, ed., *The Iran-Contra Scandal: The Declassified History* (New York, N.Y.: The New Press and National Security Archive, 1993), 408–11.

7. University of Virginia Miller Center (Charlottesville), George H. W. Bush Oral History Project, "Proving Ground: How the December 1989 invasion of Panama shaped the Bush 41 foreign policy team," undated.

8. Marianne LeVine, "Trump calls political enemies 'vermin,' echoing dictators Hitler, Mussolini," *The Washington Post* (November 12, 2023).

*Chapter One*

1. William Stanley, *The Protection Racket State: Elite Politics, Military Extortion, and Civil War in El Salvador* (Philadelphia, Pa.: Temple University Press, 1996), 222–23.

2. William M. LeoGrande, *Our Own Backyard: The United States and Central America, 1977–1992* (Chapel Hill: University of North Carolina Press, 1998), 165.

3. Stanley, *The Protection Racket State*, 120–21.

4. LeoGrande, *Our Own Backyard*, 86–88.

5. Julia Preston, "U.S. Deports Salvadoran General Accused in '80s Killings," *The New York Times* (April 8, 2015): 8A.

*Chapter Two*

1. Americas Watch, *El Salvador's Decade of Terror: Human Rights since the Assassination of Archbishop Romero* (New Haven, Conn.: Yale University Press, 1991), 146.

2. Raymond Bonner, *Weakness and Deceit: U.S. Policy and El Salvador* (New York, NY: Times Books, 1984), 61–62; and William M. LeoGrande, *Our Own Backyard: The United States and Central America, 1977–1992* (Chapel Hill: University of North Carolina Press, 1998), 48–49.

3. Bonner, *Weakness and Deceit*, 239–40, and Americas Watch, *El Salvador's Decade of Terror*, 12.

*Chapter Three*

1. Greg Grandin, *The Last Colonial Massacre: Latin America in the Cold War, Updated Edition* (Chicago, Ill.: University of Chicago Press, 2011), 127.

2. Corrine B. Johnson, "Guatemala's 'bum rap'?" *Christian Science Monitor* (January 6, 1983).

3. Inter-American Commission on Human Rights, Organization of American States, "Report on the Situation of Human Rights in the Republic of Guatemala" (October 13, 1981).

4. Scott Wallace, "Quiet war roots out Guatemala guerrillas," *The Atlanta Journal-Constitution* (September 26, 1983): 33A.

5. Scott Wallace, "Support won with terror," *The Guardian* (July 13, 1989).

6. Olivia Carrescia, director, "Todos Santos: The Survivors" (Icarus Films, 1989).

7. United States Institute of Peace, "Truth Commission: Guatemala" (February 1, 1997).

8. Peter Canby, "Death Squad Dossier," *New York Review of Books* (December 8, 2022): 10–14.

Caught off-guard, a U.S. military advisor (center left), disguised in hat and camouflage paint, disembarks with an M-16 rifle with Salvadoran government troops, San Pedro Perulapán, Cuscatlán Department, El Salvador, August 1983. With memories from Vietnam still present, U.S. military personnel were prohibited from taking part in combat operations.

9. Douglas Farrah, "Papers Show U.S. Role in Guatemalan Abuses," *The Washington Post* (March 11, 1999): A26.

10. Kate Doyle and Carlos Osorio, "U.S. Policy in Guatemala, 1966–1996" (Washington, DC: The National Security Archive, 2000): https://nsarchive2.gwu.edu/NSAEBB/NSAEBB32/vol2.html.

*Chapter Four*

1. Americas Watch, *El Salvador's Decade of Terror: Human Rights since the Assassination of Archbishop Romero* (New Haven, Conn.: Yale University Press, 1991), 145; and Fátima Peña, "Estados Unidos supo de la masacre de La Quesera y no retiró ayuda a la Fuerza Armada," *El Faro* (December 16, 2015); https://elfaro.net/es/201512/el_salvador/17643/Estados-Unidos-supo-de-la-masacre-de-La-.

2. Neil Sheehan, *A Bright Shining Lie: John Paul Van and America in Vietnam* (New York, N.Y.: Vintage Books, 1989), 207–08, 308–10, 373–74.

*Chapter Five*

1. Joan Didion, *Salvador* (New York, N.Y.: Simon and Schuster, 1983), 95; and William M. LeoGrande, *Our Own Backyard: The United States and Central America, 1977–1992* (Chapel Hill: University of North Carolina Press, 1998), 444.

2. Americas Watch, *El Salvador's Decade of Terror*, 47–48.

3. Scott Wallace, "Salvadoran peasants recall terror of army assault," *The Atlanta Journal-Constitution* (September 16, 1984): 1A.

4. Scott Wallace, "Hueys in El Salvador: Preparing for a Stepped-Up War?" *The Nation* (October 20, 1984): 377–78.

5. James S. Corum, "The Air War in El Salvador," *Air Power Journal*, Vol. 12, No. 2 (Summer 1998): 33–35.

6. Marcos Alemán, "Salvador Court Orders Arrests in Dutch Journalists Killings," Associated Press (October 16, 2022)

7. Americas Watch, *El Salvador's Decade of Terror,* 52.

*Chapter Six*

1. William M. LeoGrande, *Our Own Backyard: The United States and Central America, 1977–1992* (Chapel Hill: University of North Carolina Press, 1998), 364–65.

2. Reed Brody, *Contra Terror in Nicaragua* (Boston, Mass.: South End Press, 1985), 12.

3. David Hoffman and Joanne Omang, "Reagan Attacks 'Totalitarian' Nicaragua in Push for Rebel Aid," *The Washington Post* (July 19, 1984).

4. Raymond Bonner, *Weakness and Deceit: U.S. Policy and El Salvador* (New York, N.Y.: Times Books, 1984), 255–57; and LeoGrande, *Our Own Backyard*, 86–89.

5. Greg Grandin, *Empire's Workshop: Latin America, the United States, and the Rise of the New Imperialism* (New York, N.Y.: Henry Holt., 2010), 116.

6. Sam Dillon, *Comandos: The CIA and Nicaragua's Contra Rebels* (New York, N.Y.: Henry Holt, 1991), 21–22.

7. LeoGrande, *Our Own Backyard*, 308.

8. LeoGrande, *Our Own Backyard*, 330–32.

9. Neil Sheehan, *A Bright Shining Lie: John Paul Van and America in Vietnam* (New York, N.Y.: Vintage Books, 1989), 376–77.

10. Stephen Kinzer, *Blood of Brothers: Life and War in Nicaragua* (New York, N.Y.: G. P. Putnam's Sons, 1991), 303.

11. Lynn Horton, *Peasants in Arms: War and Peace in the Mountains of Nicaragua, 1979–1994* (Athens: Ohio University Center for International Studies, 1998), 181–84.

12. Scott Wallace, "Coffee perking up Nicaraguan economy," *The Atlanta Journal-Constitution* (February 9, 1986): 18A.
13. Sheehan, *A Bright Shining Lie,* 540–42.

*Chapter Seven*

1. Stephen Kinzer, *Blood of Brothers: Life and War in Nicaragua* (New York, N.Y.: G. P. Putnam's Sons, 1991), 253–54.

2. Scott Wallace, "The Guns Fall Silent on the Miskito Coast," *Grand Street*, Vol. 7, No. 3 (Spring 1988): 115–16.

3. Frederick Kempe and Clifford Krauss, " U.S. Policy on Indians in Nicaragua Damages Anti-Sandinista Effort," *The Wall Street Journal* (March 2, 1987): 1A.

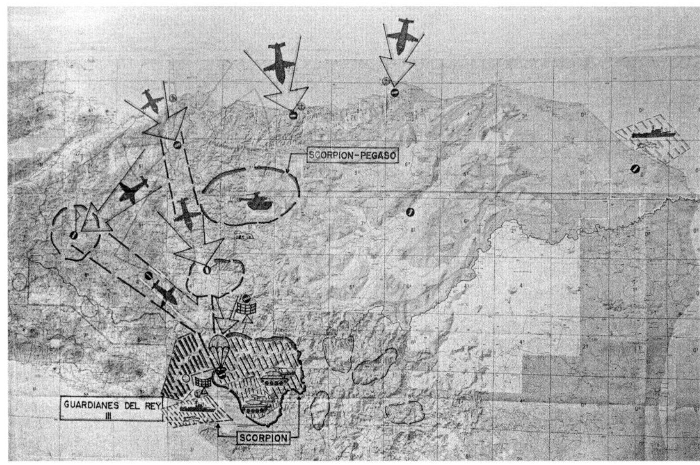


Photo of a map showing U.S. military maneuvers in support of the Honduran military and the Contra rebels displayed at a Nicaraguan Defense Ministry press conference, Managua, Nicaragua, April 1985. During the 1980s, the U.S. conducted near-continuous air-land-sea operations and exercises in and around Honduras, building airfields and military bases. The Sandinistas and some members of the U.S. Congress understood the maneuvers to be laying the groundwork for a potential U.S. invasion of Nicaragua.

4. David Hoffman, "Reagan Visits Death Camp, Cemetery," *The Washington Post* (May 6, 1985): 6A.

5. Scott Wallace, "The Real Miskito Coast," *Newsweek* (December 15, 1986).

6. Scott Wallace, "Nicaraguan Indians seek unity in fight against Sandinistas," *The Atlanta Journal-Constitution* (September 15, 1985): 12B.

7. Holly Sklar, *Washington's War on Nicaragua* (Boston, Mass.: South End Press, 1988), 288–89.

8. Scott Wallace, "Sandinistas seeking peace with Miskitos," *The Atlanta Journal-Constitution* (September 29, 1985): 40A.

9. Joel Brinkley, "Contra Arms Crews Said to Smuggle Drugs," *The New York Times* (January 20, 1987): 1A.

10. Wallace, "The Guns Fall Silent," 113–14.

*Chapter Eight*

1. Scott Wallace, "Hunting down the sons of Reagan," *The Independent* (May 13, 1987): 14.

2. Stephen Kinzer, "Sandinistas Report Capture of Redeye Missile," *The New York Times* (July 23, 1987): A9.

3. William M. LeoGrande, *Our Own Backyard: The United States and Central America, 1977–1992* (Chapel Hill: University of North Carolina Press, 1998), 377–80.

4. Edward Cody, "U.S. Source Tells of Spy Flights Over Nicaragua," *The Washington Post* (April 27, 1984).

5. Scott Wallace, "Nicaragua vows bloodbath if U.S. invades," *The Atlanta Constitution* (June 21, 1985).

*Chapter Nine*

1. Raymond Bonner, "America's Role in El Salvador's Deterioration," *The Atlantic* (January 20, 2018).

2. James S. Corum, "The Air War in El Salvador," *Air Power Journal*, Vol. 12, No. 2 (Summer 1998): 33–35, as quoted on 31.

3. Scott Wallace, "Hueys in El Salvador: Preparing for a Stepped-Up War?" *The Nation* (October 20, 1984): 337–78; and Corum, "The Air War in El Salvador," 33.

4. Americas Watch. *El Salvador's Decade of Terror: Human Rights Since the Assassination of Archbishop Romero* (New Haven, Conn.: Yale University Press, 1991), 68.

5. Scott Wallace, "The two electoral faces of Arena," *The Guardian* (March 17, 1989).

6. William M. LeoGrande, *Our Own Backyard: The United States and Central America, 1977–1992* (Chapel Hill: University of North Carolina Press, 1998), 86–89.

7. James LeMoyne, "Salvador Rebels: Where Do They Get the Arms?" *The New York Times* (November 24, 1988): A14.

*Chapter Ten*

1. Stephen G. Rabe, *The Killing Zone: The United States Wages Cold War in Latin America, Second Edition* (New York, N.Y.: Oxford University Press, 2016), 170.

2. Sam Dillon, *Comandos: The CIA and Nicaragua's Contra Rebels* (New York, N.Y.: Henry Holt, 1991), 169.

*Chapter Eleven*
1. E. J. Dionne, "Kicking the 'Vietnam Syndrome,'" *The Washington Post* (March 4, 1991).

2. Loren Thompson, "Iraq: The Biggest Mistake in American Military History," *Forbes* (December 15, 2011).

3. Greg Grandin, *Empire's Workshop: Latin America, the United States, and the Rise of the New Imperialism* (New York, N.Y.: Henry Holt., 2010), 230–31.

4. Thomas E. Ricks, *Fiasco: The American Military Adventure in Iraq* (New York, N.Y.: Penguin, 2006), 136.

5. Scott Wallace, "'God, I hate these people,' says the sergeant. Some utter the V-word: Vietnam," *The Independent* (July 20, 2003).

6. Scott Wallace, unpublished field notes, Bernard Kerik speaking at the Iraq Police Academy, Baghdad (July 16, 2003).

7. Walter Pincus, "Promotions of 2 North Associates Delayed in Senate," *The Washington Post* (October 16, 1986).

8. University of Virginia Miller Center, "Proving Ground: How the December 1989 invasion of Panama shaped the Bush 41 foreign policy team."

9. Nick Turse, *Kill Anything that Moves: The Real American War in Vietnam* (New York, N.Y.: Picador, 2013), 190–91.

10. Andrew Cockburn, *Kill Chain: The Rise of the High-Tech Assassins* (New York, N.Y.: Henry Holt, 2015), 87–88.

11. Turse, *Kill Anything that Moves*, 14–15.

12. William Stanley, *The Protection Racket State: Elite Politics, Military Extortion, and Civil War in El Salvador* (Philadelphia, Pa.: Temple University Press, 1996), 226; and Fátima Peña, "Estados Unidos supo de la masacre de La Quesera y no retiró ayuda a la Fuerza Armada," *El Faro* (December 16, 2015); https://elfaro.net/es/201512/el_salvador/17643/Estados-Unidos-supo-de-la-masacre-de-La-.

Sandinista militiamen, Nueva Segovia Department, Nicaragua, 1984.

Americas Watch, *El Salvador's Decade of Terror: Human Rights Since the Assassination of Archbishop Romero* (New Haven, Conn.: Yale University Press, 1991).

Anderson, Jon Lee, *The Fall of Baghdad* (New York, N.Y.: Penguin Press, 2004).

Bacevich, Andrew and Daniel A. Sjursen, ed., *Paths of Dissent: Soldiers Speak Out Against America's Misguided Wars* (New York, N.Y.: Metropolitan Books, Henry Holt, 2022).

Becker, Elizabeth, *You Don't Belong Here: How Three Women Rewrote the Story of War* (New York, N.Y.: Public Affairs, 2021).

Belli, Gioconda, trans. by Kristina Cordero, *The Country Under My Skin: A Memoir of Love and War* (New York, N.Y.: Alfred A. Knopf, 2002).

Bergen, Peter L., *The Longest War: The Enduring Conflict between America and Al-Qaeda* (New York, N.Y.: Free Press, 2011).

Black, George, *Garrison Guatemala* (New York, N.Y.: Monthly Review Press, 1984).

Blitzer, Jonathan, *Everyone Who Is Gone Is Here: The United States, Central America, and the Making of a Crisis* (New York, N.Y.: Penguin Press, 2024).

Bonner, Raymond, *Weakness and Deceit: U.S. Policy and El Salvador* (New York, N.Y.: Times Books, 1984).

Bracamonte, José Angel Moroni, and David E. Spencer, *Strategy and Tactics of the Salvadoran FMLN Guerrillas: Last Battle of the Cold War, Blueprint for Future Conflicts* (Westport, Conn.: Praeger, 1995).

Brody, Reed, *Contra Terror in Nicaragua* (Boston, Mass.: South End Press, 1985).

Ching, Erik, *Stories of the Civil War in El Salvador: A Battle Over Memory* (Chapel Hill: University of North Carolina Press, 2016).

Cockburn, Andrew, *Kill Chain: The Rise of the High-Tech Assassins* (New York, N.Y.: Henry Holt, 2015).

Cockburn, Leslie, *Out of Control: The Story of the Reagan Administration's Secret War in Nicaragua, the Illegal Arms Pipeline, and the Contra Drug Connection* (New York, N.Y.: Atlantic Monthly Press, 1987).

Consalvi, Carlos Henríquez ("Santiago"), trans. by Charles Leo Nagle V with A. L. (Bill) Prince, *Broadcasting the Civil War in El Salvador: A Memoir of Guerrilla Radio* (Austin: University of Texas Press, 2010).

Danner, Mark, *The Massacre at El Mozote* (New York, N.Y.: Vintage Books, 1994).

Didion, Joan, *Salvador* (New York, N.Y.: Simon and Schuster, 1983).

Diettes, Erika, *Memento Mori: Testament to Life* (Staunton, Va.: George F. Thompson Publishing, 2016).

Dillon, Sam, *Comandos: The CIA and Nicaragua's Contra Rebels* (New York, N.Y.: Henry Holt, 1991).

D'Haeseleer, Brian, *The Salvadoran Crucible: The Failure of U.S. Counterinsurgency in El Salvador, 1978–1992* (Lawrence: University Press of Kansas, 2017).

Draper, Robert, *To Start a War: How the Bush Administration Took America into Iraq* (New York, N.Y.: Penguin, 2020).

Falla, Ricardo, trans. by Julia Howland, *Massacres in the Jungle: Ixcán, Guatemala, 1975–1982* (Boulder, Colo.: Westview Press, 1994).

Forché, Carolyn, *What You Have Heard Is True: A Memoir of Witness and Resistance* (New York, N.Y.: Penguin Press, 2019).

Gentile, Bill, *Wait for Me: True Stories of War, Love and Rock & Roll* (Washington, D.C.: Bill Gentile, 2021).

Goldman, Francisco, *The Art of Political Murder: Who Killed the Bishop?* (New York, N.Y.: Grove Press, 2007).

González, Juan, *Harvest of Empire: A History of Latinos in America, Second Revised Edition* (New York, N.Y.: Penguin Books, 2022).

Grandin, Greg, *Empire's Workshop: Latin America, the United States, and the Rise of the New Imperialism* (New York, N.Y.: Henry Holt, 2010).

Grandin, Greg, *Kissinger's Shadow: The Long Reach of America's Most Controversial Statesman* (New York, N.Y.: Metropolitan Books, 2015).

Grandin, Greg, *The Last Colonial Massacre: Latin America in the Cold War* (Chicago, Ill.: University of Chicago Press, 2011).

Halberstam, David, *The Making of a Quagmire: America and Vietnam During the Kennedy Era, Revised Edition* (Lanham, Md.: Rowman & Littlefield, 2008).

Haggarty, Richard A., ed., *El Salvador: A Country Study* (Washington, D.C.: Government Printing Office for the Library of Congress, 1988).

Hertsgaard, Mark, *On Bended Knee: The Press and the Reagan Presidency* (New York, N.Y.: Farrar, Straus and Giroux, 1988).

Horton, Lynn, *Peasants in Arms: War and Peace in the Mountains of Nicaragua, 1979–1994* (Athens: Ohio University Center for International Studies, 1998).

Kagan, Robert, *A Twilight Struggle: American Power and Nicaragua, 1977–1990* (New York, N.Y.: Free Press, 1996).

Kinzer, Stephen, *Blood of Brothers: Life and War in Nicaragua* (New York, N.Y.: G. P. Putnam's Sons, 1991).

Kornbluh, Peter, and Malcolm Byrne, *The Iran-Contra Scandal: The Declassified History* (New York, N.Y.: The New Press and National Security Archive, 1993).

LeoGrande, William M., *Our Own Backyard: The United States and Central America, 1977–1992* (Chapel Hill: University of North Carolina Press, 1998).

Lovato, Roberto, *Unforgetting: A Memoir of Family, Migration, Gangs, and Revolution in the Americas* (New York, N.Y.: Harper Collins, 2020).

Lyon, Larry, editor, *1930: Manhattan to Managua, North America's First Transnational Automobile Trip* (Staunton, Va.: George F. Thompson Publishing, 2020).

Manz, Beatriz, *Refugees of a Hidden War: The Aftermath of Counterinsurgency in Guatemala* (Albany: State of New York University Press, 1988).

McConahay, Mary Jo, *Ricochet: Two Women War Reporters and a Friendship under Fire* (San Francisco, Calif.: Wayne Goodman Books, 2016).

Montgomery, Tommie Sue, *Revolution in El Salvador: Origins and Evolution* (Boulder, Colo.: Westview Press, 1982).

Petraeus, General David and Andrew Roberts, *Conflict: The Evolution of Warfare from 1945 to Ukraine* (New York, N.Y.: HarperCollins, 2023).

Prochnau, William, *Once Upon a Distant War* (New York, N.Y.: Times Books, 1995.)

Rabe, Stephen G., *The Killing Zone: The United States Wages Cold War in Latin America, Second Edition* (New York, N.Y.: Oxford University Press, 2016).

Ricks, Thomas E., *Fiasco: The American Military Adventure in Iraq* (New York, N.Y.: Penguin, 2006).

Risen, James, *The Last Honest Man: The CIA, the FBI, the Mafia, and the Kennedys—and One Senator's Fight to Save Democracy* (Boston, Mass.: Little, Brown and Company, 2023).

Sheehan, Neil, *A Bright Shining Lie: John Paul Vann and America in Vietnam* (New York, N.Y.: Random House, 1988).

Simon, Jean-Marie, *Guatemala: Eternal Spring, Eternal Tyranny* (New York, N.Y.: W. W. Norton, 1987).

Sklar, Holly, *Washington's War on Nicaragua* (Boston, Mass.: South End Press, 1988).

Spencer, David E., *From Vietnam to El Salvador: The Saga of the FMLN Sappers and Other Guerrilla Special Forces in Latin America* (Westport, Conn.: Praeger, 1996).

Stanley, William, *The Protection Racket State: Elite Politics, Military Extortion, and Civil War in El Salvador* (Philadelphia, Pa.: Temple University Press, 1996).

Turse, Nick, *Kill Anything that Moves: The Real American War in Vietnam* (New York, N.Y.: Picador, 2013).

Uclés, Mario Lungo, *El Salvador in the Eighties: Counterinsurgency and Revolution* (Philadelphia, Pa.: Temple University Press, 1996).

Walsh, Lawrence, *Firewall: The Iran-Contra Conspiracy and Cover-Up* (New York, N.Y.: W. W. Norton, 1997).

Whitlock, Craig, and the Washington Post, *The Afghanistan Papers: A Secret History of the War* (New York, N.Y.: Simon & Schuster, 2021).

Reuters correspondent Bobby Block (center, sitting) interviews a guerrilla, Chalatenango Department, El Salvador, 1984.

*Acknowledgments*

**L**ike any major project, this book could not have been made without the invaluable contributions of many people, especially at the University of Connecticut. It began in my early days at UConn in 2017, when I heard political science and human rights professor Shareen Hertel speak at an orientation session. I was drawn to her passion for human-rights issues and Latin America. She advised me to meet Glenn Mitoma, then-Director of UConn's Thomas J. Dodd Research Center (and now at Columbia University), and Kathryn Libal, Director of the Human Rights Institute. In a meeting with Glenn, Kathy, Graham Stinnett of UConn's Archives & Special Collections, and Nana Amos from Dodd Human Rights Impact, the idea germinated to create an exhibition of my work from Central America during the 1980s. Glenn and Kathy were prime supporters of the exhibit, entitled "In the Crosshairs: Dispatches from Central America, 1983–1990," which came to fruition in 2019, and they and the newly christened Dodd Center for Human Rights and Gladstein Family Human Rights Institute have been instrumental in making this book a reality.

The project gained momentum with the backing of Daniel Weiner, Vice President for Global Affairs, as well as the Humanities Institute and its then-Director, Michael Lynch. I counted on invaluable counsel from Dan and Michael and from UCHI's Alexis Boylan and Yohei Igarashi. Thanks, also, to Elizabeth Della Zazzera and Nasya Al-Saidy at UCHI, where I was honored with a Humanities Fellowship in 2020–2021. I have received generous support from the College of Liberal Arts and Sciences, including former Dean Juli Wade, Interim Dean Ofer Harel, and Associate Dean Evelyn Tribble. I also received generous assistance from UConn's El Instituto: Institute of Latina/o, Caribbean and Latin American Studies. Thanks especially to Samuel Martínez, Anne Gebelein, Katerina González Seligmann, and Kimberly Vásquez.

None of this would have been possible without my amazing colleagues in UConn's Department of Journalism, including former head Maureen Croteau, current head Marie Shanahan, and educational programs coordinator Lisa Caruso. Thanks to Amanda Crawford, who read parts of the book and provided valuable suggestions, as well as Mike Stanton, Julie Serkosky, Steve Kalb, Martine Granby, Gail MacDonald, Steve Smith, and emeritus faculty Bob Wyss and Marcel Dufresne. Thanks to many UConn friends from other departments for their friendship, including David Wagner, Jeremy Pressman, Heather Elliott-Famularo, Rob Venator, Robin Greeley and Michael Orwicz as well as Carol Atkinson-Palombo, César Abadía-Barrero, Jon Bauer, Gary English, Ken Foote, Mark Healey, Guillermo Irizarry, Molly Land, Catherine Masud, Gustavo Nanclares, Helen Rozwadowski, Margaret Rubega, Jennifer Schaefer, Anji Seth, Robert

Thorson, Mark Urban, Richard Wilson, Dimitris Xygalatas, and Victor Zatsepine. Thanks to student research assistant Claire Lee and Web designer Haydn Kerr. And thanks to my fabulous students who offer hope for the future with their enthusiasm for unearthing the truth in these ever more challenging times.

It was a stroke of luck that George F. Thompson visited UConn as a Publisher-in-Residence while the exhibition was hanging. He was impressed by what he saw and urged me to create a book. Little did we know then that he would publish it. I thank George, for his clarity of vision, enthusiasm, and stewardship. My thanks also to David Skolkin, for the book's beautiful design, and to Mikki Soroczak, for her tireless work blending the various iterations of text with the book's images. Cartographer Rachael H. Carpenter created a terrific map.

I owe a debt of gratitude to Carl Hoffman, who read various drafts of the manuscript and offered many incisive suggestions. Many thanks, also, to Peter Bergen, Andrew Cockburn, Michael Robinson, and Jon Lee Anderson, for reviewing the manuscript, and to Scott Anderson, Alice Elliott Dark, Bob Shacochis, Crary Pullen, Catherine Blinder, Jon Hooker, Clif Wiens, Geoff O'Connor, Jake Cunningham, as well as Bob Ahern of Getty Images, for their contributions. The photographs were edited by Greg Miller and Steve Uzzell. Thanks to Steve and his late partner, Susan Lambert, for their mentorship, as well as to Bill Gentile, Lou DeMatteis, and Robert Nickelsberg for contributing images to this book.

I worked with an incredible group of colleagues in Central America, especially Bob Nickelsberg, Jon Lee Anderson, Bill Gentile, Bobby Block, Tim Loughran, Matthew Campbell, John Carlin, Edith Coron, the late Josetxo Zaldua, Sandra García, Ingrid Arnesen, Wesley Bocxe, Miguel Real, the late Ana Padilla Real, and Arturo Robles as well as David Adams, Marcos Alemán, Arthur Allen, Michael Allen, Vivian Altman, Manny Alvarez, Roberto Alvarez, the late Cecilia Alvear, Lucia Annunziata, Ana Arana, María Cristina Arguello, Peter Arnett, Betsy Aron, María Ayala, Nelson Ayala, Claudia Baca, Alberto Barrera, Javier Bauluz, Gioconda Belli, Raúl Beltrán, Alex Benes, Jeremy Bigwood, George Black, Jason Bliebtreu, the late Paulo Bosio, Larry Boyd, Bryna Brennan, Phil Bronstein, James Brooke, the late Roger Burbach, the late Kevin Buckley, the late Any Cabrera, Daniel Caselli, Charlie Castaldi, Estella Castillo, Ricardo Castillo, Tony Cavin, Bill Clary, Lydia Chávez, Noam Chomsky, Marcelle Clements, the late Alexander Cockburn, Andrew Cockburn, Leslie Cockburn, Peter Collins, the late Tim Coone, Joe Contreras, Marc Cooper, the late Donato Coppola, Chris and Lucinda Covert-Vail, Randy Credico, Emma Daly, Bernd Debusmann, Mario de Carvalho, Donna DeCesare, Manoocher Deghati, Lou Dematteis, Paco de Onís, the late Luis Díaz, the late Chris Dickey, Sam Dillon, Paula Dobbyn, Steven Donziger, Alister Doyle, Mike Drudge, Kees Elenbaas, the late Paul Ellman, June Erlick, Rafael Escobar, Doug Farah, Carla Farrell, Jean-Jacques Feron, Bill Finnegan, Patricia Flynn, Peter Ford, Joe Frazier, Luis Galdámez, Joe Gannon, the late Anne Garrels, Rob Gentile, Tom Gibb, Tom Gjelten, Lenny Glynn, Paul Goepfert, Tim Golden, Frank Goldman, David Gollob, Bill Goodfellow, Michael Gregor, Lindsey Gruson, Arturo Gudiño, Joy Hackel, Don Hamilton, the late Pat Hamilton, Ron Haviv, Annelies Helwegen, Lee Hockstader, David Holiday, Cookie Hood, Lucy Hood, the late Laura Hurtado, Pablo Iacub, Epigmenio Ibarra, Tony Jenkins, the late Paul Kantner, Cindy Karp, the late Ron Kinney, Cliff Krauss, Adam Kufeld, John Lantigua, the late Cornel Lagrouw, Susan Leffler, James Lemoyne, Malcom Linton, Ronnie Lovler, Robin Lubbock, Angus MacSwan, the late Frank Manitzas, Mary Jo McConahay, Peter McCormick, Nancy McGirr, Chris McGreal, Maureen Meehan, Susan Meiselas, Luis Alfredo Mejía, Rafael Mejía, Marjorie Miller, Reid Miller, Iván Montecinos, Sofía Montenegro, Roberto and Viviana Moreno, Maria Morrison, Matthew Naythons, Anne Nelson, Lucia Newman, James Nachtwey, Nancy Nusser,

Annie O'Connor, the late Mike O'Connor, María Lourdes Pallais, Gene Palumbo, Gilles Peress, the late Jeff Perkell, Blanche Petrich, the late Roberto Pineda, the late Christian Poveda, Julia Preston, Oscar Ramírez, Domingo Rex, Dan Riesenfeld, William Ring, Bob Rivard, Jaime Robles, Luis Romero, the late Carlos Rosas, Tim Ross, the late J. Randolph "Ry" Ryan, Angela Saballos, Jan Schmeitz, Andrew Selsky, Monica Seoane, David Shanahan, Janet Shenk, the late Leroy Sievers, Laurie Singer, Frank Smyth, Mary Speck, Sharon Stevenson, Les Stone, Michele Taverna, the late Manlio Tirado, the late Alan Tomlinson, the late Doug Tweedale, Alba Valle, Jan Van Bilsen, the late Dirk Van Der Sypen, Juan Vasquez, Patricia Vasquez, the late Richard Wagner, the late Ian Walker, Martin Walker, Tracy Wilkinson, Pamela Yates, Marcello Zanini, and the late Erico Zas. Special thanks to John Harris, Larry McCoy, and Susan Zirinsky at CBS and to the late Randal Ashley of *The Atlanta Journal-Constitution*.

A big thank you to Senator Dodd, for his service to the American people, his immeasurable contributions to the vitality of the University of Connecticut community, and his courageous opposition to the war policies of the Reagan-Bush Administrations during the 1980s. And, of course, for agreeing to write the foreword for *Central America in the Crosshairs of War.*

My thanks and love to my three sons: Mackenzie, Aaron, and Ian. Much of their personal story is bound up with this one. And to my wife and partner, Meg Walsh. With love and gratitude.

Scott Wallace with Miskito rebels, Yulu, Nicaragua, November 1986. Photograph © Bill Gentile and used by permission.

**Scott Wallace** (b. 1954) is an award-winning writer, photographer, and broadcast producer who has covered vanishing cultures, armed conflict, and the environment for the past four decades. A long-time contributor to *National Geographic*, Wallace reported from Central America during the 1980s for CBS News, CNN, *The Atlanta Journal-Constitution*, *The Guardian*, *The Independent*, and *Newsweek*. His articles have also appeared in *The Washington Post*, *The Village Voice*, *Smithsonian*, *Smithsonian Journeys Quarterly*, *The New York Times*, *The Nation*, *National Geographic Adventure*, *Harper's*, *Interview*, *Grand Street*, and *Condé Nast Traveler*. His photography, represented by Getty Images, has been published in magazines and newspapers throughout the world, including *The Wall Street Journal*, *Smithsonian*, *Outside*, *The New York Times*, *National Geographic*, *National Geographic Traveler*, *The Guardian*, *The Economist*, and *Details*. His first book, *The Unconquered: In Search of the Amazon's Last Uncontacted Tribes* (Crown, 2011; paperback, Broadway, 2012), was a *New York Times* bestseller.

Wallace's assignments have taken him from the Pamir and Hindu Kush of Afghanistan to the jungles of South America and from the Norwegian Arctic to the lowlands of Bangladesh. He has reported on the rise of organized crime in post-Soviet Russia, the controversy surrounding oil development on Alaska's North Slope, and efforts to stem wildlife trafficking in Myanmar.

Wallace has been honored with the Explorers Club's Lowell Thomas Award, for excellence in reporting from the field, and received awards from the Associated Press, Gannett Newspapers, Inter-American Press Association, Renewable Natural Resources Foundation, Society of American Travel Writers, and Society of Professional Journalists. Wallace is an associate professor of journalism at the University of Connecticut.

**Christopher J. Dodd** was born in 1944 in Willimantic, Connecticut. He earned a B.A. in English literature from Providence College and received his J.D. from the Brandeis School of Law at the University of Louisville. From 1966 to 1968 he was a Peace Corps volunteer in the Dominican Republic, and from 1969 to 1975 he served in the U.S. Army Reserve. Dodd then became Connecticut's longest-serving member of Congress, first as a member of the House of Representatives from 1975 to 1981 and then the U.S. Senate from 1981 to 2011. Upon retirement from the U.S. Senate in 2011, Senator Dodd became Chairman and CEO of the Motion Picture Association of America, and, in 2018, he joined the law firm of Arnold & Porter as a Senior Counsel. Senator Dodd also served as Special Advisor on the Americas to President Joseph R. Biden. He and his wife, Jackie Clegg Dodd, have two daughters and reside in East Haddam, Connecticut.

Scott Wallace's desk, Guatemala City, Guatemala, 1989.

*Central America in the Crosshairs of War: On the Road from Vietnam to Iraq* was brought to publication in an edition of 800 hardcover copies. The text was set in Century Old Style and Din, the paper is Kinmari Dull-Ex, 157 gsm weight, and the book was professionally printed and bound by Pristone Printing, Ltd., in Singapore.

Publisher: George F. Thompson
Editorial and Research Assistant: Mikki Soroczak
Manuscript Editor: Purna Makaram
Book Design and Production: David Skolkin
Photo Editor: Greg Miller

*Special Acknowledgments*: The publisher extends grateful thanks and appreciation to Richard Misrach, for his wise counsel and encouragement, and to the University of Connecticut's College of Liberal Arts and Sciences, Dodd Center for Human Rights, Gladstein Family Human Rights Institute, Office of Global Affairs, Humanities Institute, El Instituto, and the Department of Journalism, for their generous support in making this project possible.

This book originated with Scott Wallace's 2019 exhibition at UConn's Dodd Center entitled "In the Crosshairs: Dispatches from Central America: 1983–1990." Small portions of this book previously appeared in *ReVista*, *Mizzou*, and *Grand Street*.

Published in 2024. First hardcover edition.
Printed in Singapore on acid-free paper.

George F. Thompson Publishing, L.L.C.
217 Oak Ridge Circle
Staunton, VA 24401–3511, U.S.A.
www.gftbooks.com

33 32 31 30 29 28 27 26 25 24     1 2 3 4 5

The Library of Congress Preassigned Control Number is 2023952143.

ISBN: 978-1-960521-01-9

# In the Nicaraguan forest, a Kalashnikov is star

TEN armed government workers rode a pick-up truck into an ambush laid by Contra rebels last week on a stretch of road appropriately named *El Infierno*. All but two of the men were mowed down in a hail of bullets, the latest victims in a savage war where the line between civilian and combatant is often blurred beyond recognition.

By that afternoon Managua radio stations were ... denunciations of "yet another ... and cowardly" Contra assault ... Nicaraguan civilians.

Obviously eager to publicise the attack, the Defence Ministry summoned reporters the next day for a trip to this frontier town some 170 miles south-east of the capital.

But interviews with the two survivors of the shooting revealed that the victims — all employees of a local state-run timber firm — were not exactly defenceless civilians, as the central government apparently had been led to believe from initial field reports. The logging crew were armed and uniformed as they rode to their deaths in search of choice trees in the forests surrounding Nueva Guinea.

According to Juan Antonio Diaz, one of the survivors, the workers were raked with machine-gun fire as they rounded a bend in the road at El Infierno, so named because of the weird twisted shapes of the surrounding hills where the Contra rebels lay in ambush.

Mr Diaz and one of his companions managed to jump from the truck and return fire with their AK-47 rifles. They broke and fled when their ammunition ran out.

The ambush once again raised troubling questions regarding the arming of civilian workers assigned to government projects in Nicaragua's hinterlands against violence by Contra rebels. Contra leaders claim that armed government workers, as well as peasant militiamen who defend their agricultural co-operatives against rebel attacks, are legitimate targets of their military operations. It would seem their assertion is, in part, backed by internationally-recognised rules of war.

**From Scott Wallace**
in Nueva Guinea, Nicaragua

Sandinista officials and government workers who carry weapons in the backwoods say the practice is necessary to prevent the Contras from abducting the rural population and paralysing Nicaragua's development. They say the Contras attack civilian and production centres to demoralise the population and roll back revolutionary social change in the countryside.

Mr Diaz said he and his fellow workers voluntarily take weapons into the fields to keep the logging project going and thereby provide a livelihood for their families and the com...

"We are defending ou... the rights of our children... said When asked if the a... deter him from continuing... gerous business, he stoic... "We must move forward ... rale on high."

Since October 1984, the ... terprise, known as the Ca... Amador Lumber Compan... 23 of its workers killed an... in Contra ambushes. Mr D... he had survived three big ...

The top Sandinista offic... gion, Wilfredo Barreto, s... of the war required the C... tempt to halt the forestry ...

---



## Preparing for a Stepped-Up War?

SCOTT WALLACE

*San Salvador*

When ten new UH-1H combat helicopters arrived here from the United States in early September, reporters were looking the other way. Yet the Vietnam-era Hueys represented

## Salvadoran peasants recall t

**By Scott Wallace**
Cox News Service

SANTA LUCIA, El Salvador — For more than two days Julio Cartagena and his family fled for their lives along with hundreds of other peasants and a small group of armed guerrillas as government troops stalked them through the gullies and cornfields of this rugged mountainous area.

*Cox Newspapers Central Ame... spondent Scott Wallace was one ... porters who managed to reach Ch... province last week to investigate ... an army atrocity. This is his report...*

and children, fled their adobe hom... lage of El Tamarindo in panic ...

---

# GIs learn how to fight the next US war in

AMID growing alarm that the United States could be faced with multiple left-

"But we tell the troops not to just blow some guy away either. That's not very

## From Farm to Fortress

### Managua expropriates land to battle the contras

For Carlos Briceño and his wife, Gloria, their 700-acre coffee farm in northern Nicaragua represented years of effort and a place to retire. But five months ago, the farm's overseer arrived at the couple's comfortable bungalow, 90 miles from the farm, bringing bad news: squatters were moving onto the property. Briceño immedi-

sion is now subject to a case-by-case review, enabling Managua officials to expropriate any land where an overriding "social interest" is at stake. Of the nearly 400 expropriations scheduled for this year—affecting some 260,000 acres—some are indeed cases where owners have largely abandoned operations. But for the Briceños and many

**From Scott Wallace** in Panama

## 'Small war' turns nigh

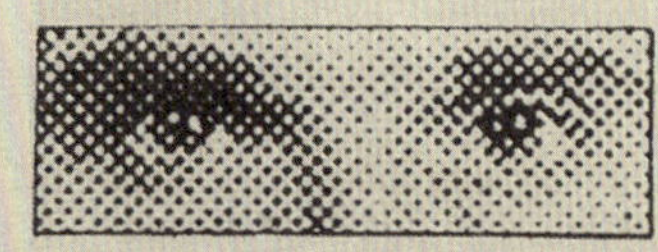

**Eyewitness**

We bounced up the road towards San Francisco Javier for about half an hour from the Pan-American highway. Peasants warned us to hold back, telling us it was still going on, which, of course, for a journalist is like a green light. We drove

and we were talking to when another car-lo journalists arrived.

It was a Dutch crew nel Lagrouw, a camer with the Dutch ch broadcasting network, with his wife, Annelise was also his sound p